INSIDE
COLLEGE
PUBLISHING

JEAN SMITH

JEAN SMITH ASSOCIATES / NEW YORK

ISBN 0-9651261-1-0
Printed in the United States of America

Cover design by Lydia Gershey of Communigraph

Statistics for the Higher Education Division used
by permission of the Association of American
Publishers.

Jean Smith Associates
100 Bank St., Suite 1D
New York, NY 10014

Phone: 212-929-4070
Fax: 212-242-0130
E-mail: JSAgents@AOL.com

CONTENTS

3 PRODUCTION & MANUFACTURING/42

PREFACE

Educational publishing is an accidental career that nabs a remarkably large and talented flock of people while they're on their way to writing the Great American novel. Because it is also a relatively invisible field, many aspects of their newfound profession remain quite mysterious, even to them.

As a manager of such folk for several decades, I find that the better the people in this industry understand it, the more successful they are in their jobs and the more fun they have. This foundation of understanding is especially critical now, during this time of radical transition.

Inside College Publishing grew out of training programs and seminars developed for brand-new sales representatives and editors, for experienced executives, for college store managers, and for students in publishing programs at major universities. After giving an overview of the industry, *Inside College Publishing* traces the steps from idea to product to marketing, with practical explanations and suggestions, anecdotes and case study material. Each chapter is a self-contained "mini-seminar" designed to lay the foundation for success in an industry in transition.

The future of this industry is going to depend on the commitment of the people going into it. *Inside College Publishing* is a starter kit toward that goal.

Jean Smith
January 1996

1 INTRODUCTION TO AN INDUSTRY

Over the years, whenever people have begun to discuss publishing for the higher education market, I've been reminded of one of the classic stories about Mulla Nasrudin, a man in the Middle East who was both a wise man and a fool. One night, a group of Nasrudin's friends were walking through the village when they spotted him across the street, near a streetlight, down on his hands and knees. They crossed over and asked him what was the matter, and he explained that he had lost the key to his house and was looking for it. Nasrudin's friends got down on their hands and knees and began to search too. But no one could find the key. Finally, one friend asked Nasrudin if he was sure he had lost the key *here*. "Oh, no," Nasrudin replied, "I lost it near my house." "Then why are we looking here?" the friend asked. "Because the light is so much better here," replied Nasrudin.

Instead of being limited to only what is most easily visible—the *products*, usually books, that are almost always the focus when college publishing is being discussed—we're going to take a spotlight to where the keys to this industry really are—the *processes* through which college publishers add unique value to those products. This role is extremely different from trade, or general, publishing. An old— and very exemplary—story relates how the manuscript for *Auntie Mame* was rejected by more than twenty publishers before it was put under contract, later to become a bestselling book, movie, and Broadway show. The game of chance that often lies behind sudden runaway bestsellers from new fiction writers almost never is played out in educational publishing. In this marketplace, there are virtually no surprises. Consider the market variables a publisher knows when bringing out a new package for, say, introductory psychology:

- The finite size of the market (introductory psychology has 1.3 million students)

- The organization that must be presented (it begins with the biological bases of behavior, then goes to learning)

- The number and names of competitive offerings (companies including McGraw-Hill, Harcourt Brace, Prentice Hall, Harper-Collins, and Allyn & Bacon bring out as many as twenty new editions a year)

- The selling strategies needed (a huge ancillary package with multimedia materials and a good computerized testing program)

- The attitude of the buyer (most of the professors making the decision would rather be teaching an upper-level course in their specialty)
- The content

The core knowledge of this discipline is not going to change, so the key to success lies in appearing to do what everyone else is doing, but to do it *qualitatively* better. How different this situation is from bringing out a new novel by Stephen King or by a writer no one has ever heard of. At the very least, someone in a trade store may well buy several novels, but no professor will have students buy more than one introductory psychology textbook for class use. It's hard enough to get them to buy one.

The central product in educational publishing has long been the textbook, but this is a time of transition when the primary delivery medium for many types of educational material will soon be electronic. But no matter what changes new technologies may bring in the delivery of these materials, it is still the publishers who must develop the pedagogically sound and appropriate content that will end up in a book or on a disk or online. For no matter how many electronic bells and whistles a new project has, if it isn't a superior teaching tool, it will be rejected.

There's a top photo agent who always sends her photographers out to shoot photo essays, even when the commission is for a single shot, because she always gets the best picture when it's taken in context. Our examination begins by giving an overview of the context of college publishing, then discussing how texts and other media come into being, with a special look at different roles, then a look to the future. In later chapters, we'll examine in depth the major areas in the processes that make up college publishing.

An Invisible Industry

Over a period of years, I asked more than 700 students enrolled in the Radcliffe Publishing Course—a distinguished summer program that attracts many of the most talented young people entering book, magazine, and multimedia publishing—how many of them grew up with a burning desire to go into college publishing. They were a fairly representative group: over the years, two people raised their hands, though in fact many of the Radcliffe graduates end up in educational publishing. Ironically, few of the people who have entered this industry originally set out to do so. Nevertheless, no matter how we get here, most of us stay.

Educational publishing is so big and employs so many people that the lack of knowledge about it is quite remarkable. Every source of numbers on the size of publishing segments seems to come up with different statistics, but no matter which source is cited, publishers who publish materials used in education—text, reference, software, etc.—together account for a huge chunk of the publishing dollar pie:

Estimated 1994 Book Sales (AAP)

College	11.6%
Educational (other than college)	14.0%
Trade	29.2%
Religious	5.2%
Professional	19.2%
Mass Market	7.4%
Other	13.4%

Sales of college educational materials amount to more than $2 billion per year. And these numbers do not reflect the millions of dollars spent on such electronic products as word-processing programs and reference CD-ROMs that are sold in ways that cannot easily be tracked.

So why is this entire industry so invisible out there in the world at large? One big factor is media coverage. When was the last time you saw a story about college publishing in your local newspaper? Even in industry publications like *Publishers Weekly*, stories are invariably about trade publishers. Why? **Advertising**.

Put simply: Trade publishers buy advertising, and college publishers do not—

for a very important reason: The people who buy a college book or disk don't choose it; a professor does. There simply are not going to be any surprise bestsellers in the educational market, because, by definition, virtually all product is designed to fit an *existing* course market.

But there's a broader issue: **Interest**. In its life, a calculus text may earn more money than a Stephen King novel (at least for book sales; the movie rights for calculus books literally go for nothing). But most people waiting in an airport would rather be reading King. The fact that they may choose to read a book that interests or distracts or amuses them is an option that students don't have for their formal studies. Once again, such choice is related to that most basic characteristic of this industry: a professor makes a decision and tells students what to buy.

A comparable industry is pharmaceuticals, in which a manufacturer gives out samples and convinces a physician of the efficacy of a drug, the physician gives patients a prescription, and patients purchase the drug from a retail store. (Parenthetically, there's an analog to generic drugs, too: used books. Publishers pay huge costs for research and development and for convincing the professor that a particular product is best, but students often buy used books, ostensibly because of price.)

Let's look more closely at the college publishing industry, first touching on an array of factors that help to shape it. We'll briefly look at:

- Concentration and specialization of publishers
- Traditional products and new technologies
- Multiple customers
- Demographics and growth patterns
- Windows of opportunity
- Price and value perception

Concentration and Specialization of Publishers

Despite publishers' relative anonymity in the world at large, several years ago, educational publishers began to get considerable play in the media because of the coverage of mergers and acquisitions. This activity slowed down for a while, but we're now in a phase where some of the companies that had acquired others have themselves been acquired. Two examples: Scott Foresman absorbed the college division of Little, Brown; but then Scott was absorbed into HarperCollins, which was put on the block in late 1995. Also, the Macmillan college division absorbed Merrill, then itself became part of Prentice Hall. When the mergers and acquisitions have been "pure publishing" deals—and that kind is rarer and rarer—the competition to acquire is almost never because of trade books except for the rare companies that have a strong backlist of "classics." (Trade books have a shelf life of about 90 days, if they're lucky, and the people who create them often jump from house to house. By contrast, successful college texts with timely revisions have stayed in the marketplace for decades.) In fact, most of the companies in the news for several years—like Simon & Schuster/ Viacom—have major interests in popular entertainment *and* in educational publishing as well.

The result of this trend is that in recent years sales have been concentrated among increasingly fewer college publishers. Although there may be 300–400 companies publishing something for this market, more than 80 percent of all sales are made by fewer than ten companies.

Largest College Publishers in 1995 *(alphabetically)*

Addison Wesley (Benjamin/ Cummings, Longman)
Harcourt Brace ([Holt], Dryden, Saunders)
HarperCollins [Scott Foresman, Little Brown]
Houghton Mifflin (D.C. Heath)
International Thomson (Wadsworth, PWS, Southwestern, Brooks-Cole)
McGraw-Hill [Random House]
Simon & Schuster (Allyn & Bacon, Prentice Hall, [Macmillan {Merrill}])
Times Mirror (Irwin, Mosby, WC Brown, Brown & Benchmark)
Wiley

$$= \pm 80\% \text{ of college sales}$$

As you can see in this alphabetical list, the names of companies in parentheses are subsidiaries or imprints of the large companies, but those in brackets have disappeared as college imprints.

This concentration into the hands of a few giants has had major impact on many aspects of educational publishing, including what materials are published and how they are sold. One notable aspect is that large companies get economies of scale, especially in sales and marketing, so they have tended to concentrate on large, unit-adoption markets where intensive personal selling efforts are needed. (Parenthetically, when two large publishers merge, the "new" company often has an abundance of introductory books—one publisher found itself with eight texts for the same introductory course, definitely too much of a good thing.)

Conversely, the smallest companies, with small sales staffs, tend to go after limited, easily identifiable markets and to rely more heavily on direct mail and journal advertising than on personal selling. At this point, the concentration among fewer publishers seems to have increased the competition at the introductory level—in many ways, improving the products presented.

Traditional Products and the New Technologies

A great deal has been said in a great many forums about the use of new technologies in higher education. Rather than being overly expansive about what we all know, let me just highlight some key points:

- The traditional product, the textbook, has long been the best portable retrieval vehicle for the knowledge in a given course.

- Other technologies have been introduced along the way, such as film and video, computerized testing, simulations.

- Innovations in technology make possible many exciting new ways to teach *and* to learn.

- What is possible far exceeds what is being used.

- What is being used is limited by economic considerations, technical expertise, and habit.

In all probability, the best of the new technologies now being used for teaching will be linked to the best of those now being used for learning in new kinds of configurations, often networked, sometimes at distant locations. What the delivery mechanisms will be even five years from now is anyone's guess. There are only two relative certainties: First, they will need the publishers for pedagogically sound presentation of content; and, second, there will still be books—the paperless classroom is about as likely as the paperless bathroom.

Multiple Customers

No matter what size a publisher is, it still has a marketplace with three customers—the professor, the student, and the college store—all of whom have needs to satisfy. Let's consider each customer briefly:

- **The professor** seeks a product for classroom use that is comprehensive, up to date, accurate, user friendly, relatively inexpensive, accompanied by an ancillary package appropriate for that course, presented by a sales representative who is knowledgeable about both the course and the product for it.

- **The student** also seeks a product that is user friendly and one that will present the information that he or she needs (a) to pass the course and (b) perhaps to lay a good foundation for further study or for employment. The cost of this information is a major factor in this customer's satisfaction.

- **The college store** seeks a number of things that could be summarized as service: accurate and timely information about publications, prompt delivery of materials, good and easy communications with both the sales representative and the company's order department; pricing or discounts that maximize profits.

In some cases, to satisfy one customer is to incur the displeasure of another. For example, the free ancillary packages required by many faculty raise the price of a text to the student.

Demographics and Growth Patterns

One factor that is having increasing impact on this marketplace—one not too often discussed—is demographics. Demographic factors such as the large shift in student population to states like Florida, Texas, and California; the numbers of students approaching college age, and the likelihood of whether they'll attend college; the older student body; and the probable resulting increase in "distance" learning will affect the kinds of educational materials created and where and how they are marketed.

Demographic studies indicate that the number of students who will be high-school age in the next decade is increasing slightly, with a modest wave that will pass through by the late 1990s. But who are these students? In many instances they are living in the South and Southwest and may be the first in their families to graduate from high school. If they continue their formal education, they may be seeking courses with emphases on career preparation.

Because of education-funding changes at the federal and state levels, students are increasingly attending local two-year and four-year institutions.

Also, the number of older students and students who are extending the time they take to get degrees is creating a demand for greater flexibility in when, where, and how they take courses. It also affects pricing: many of these householders are supporting families as well as studies, and they, especially, may seek the least-expensive options for course materials.

Although the growth curve for print products has been relatively flat in recent years, the sales of nonprint items and services are showing quite a different pattern. As the deliverers of content, publishers are quite optimistic about opportunities with these changing demographics.

Windows of Opportunity

One factor that greatly affects publishers internally is the relatively short period during which most adoption decisions are made. It's like the space program: there's a narrow launch window at a specific time, and if you miss it, you don't go into orbit. You either scrub the mission or end up lost in outer space. Similarly, publishers must get a new edition into the hands of potential adopters during that window or they have no chance of getting the adoption for at least a term, perhaps for several years, perhaps never.

As a result, unlike other kinds of publishing, all textbooks for a given year go through the same cycles at about the same time. This means, for example, that all the major textbooks for all college publishers must be printed during the same period. So even before the competition for adoptions, there's some competition for press time at the relatively few printers who can do big full-color texts. Sales representatives for all companies in all disciplines close a very great proportion of their annual business in the same short period of time.

Interestingly, some of the new technologies seem to affect this pattern. Some nonprint products—especially supplements—may be adopted at almost any time. The new "live," online products, too, are not limited by these cycles. The "windows" may be turning into glass classrooms.

Price and Value Perception

Every issue mentioned so far affects the price of educational materials. The other major factor in pricing that hasn't directly come up is the result of used books. A number of years ago, publishers had a fairly clear picture of sales patterns and budgeted, for example, how costs would be amortized over the life of an edition; the second-year and third-year falloff pattern from used books and from professors changing texts was predictable. The aggressive activities of used-book sellers increased over time and the falloff after the first year became steeper. But today these activities are severely affecting first-year sales. Consider two recent examples, both in the **first** year of publication:

1. An introductory psychology textbook was adopted by a two-year college that had 1,200 students enrolled in the course; the free ancillary package that went to each instructor was worth several hundred dollars. But only 200 texts were ordered by the college store, and a few of those were returned. The math is simple: more than a thousand copies of this brand-new book—

five times as many as were bought—were gotten from a source other than the publisher.

2. A state university sent out a legalish form requiring that publishers, to be eligible for adoptions, guarantee that desk copies would be provided to all instructors, no matter how many student copies were ordered. This university adopted three books from the same publisher for its freshman English composition course, which enrolled more than a thousand students; instead of ordering some 3,000 books, they ordered 300 handbooks and fewer than 200 each of two readers—again, all books in their first year.

This cannibalizing of *first*-year sales is devastating to the profitability of publishers and makes them question both how and what they publish *and* how they distribute. Also, in the second case, the publisher practically had to threaten the sales representative to get him back on that campus, because he felt he lost sales at other campuses while he spent time creating sales for a "used-book" dealer. The ethical and legal questions surrounding how those "used" copies were obtained is beyond the scope of this book.

The point is that the same attitude that marks trafficking in books as a commodity for the highest profit is communicated to students when they get pressured by "used-book wholesalers" at the end of a semester to "Lose twenty ugly pounds: sell us your books." Such campaigns devalue the educational material and, by extension, the education. You simply can't put down the core knowledge of a discipline as "twenty ugly pounds" without implying that the knowledge as well as the book has little lasting worth. This denigration of the educational process itself is destructive to everyone.

Used books will be in the marketplace as long as books are. But the *first* sale of books by parties other than publishers will inevitably force publishers to find other ways to distribute their materials—ways and media that return fair compensation to authors and to owners. In at least one instance, this has involved selling directly to students.

Underlying factors such as demographics and new technologies are extraordinarily complex and are changing rapidly. Nevertheless, these challenges are also providing publishers with a number of opportunities. With this background, let's look at how companies are structured, then at how works come to be published.

Who Does What?

There is no one diagram that fits all publishers. In some cases, such as a small company, all departments report to a president or general manager. When college publishers are part of larger corporations, functions such as accounting, warehousing, and manufacturing may be part of separate, centralized units that service the whole corporation.

With those qualifications, let me outline the major areas of responsibility as they exist in most publishing companies. Each will be examined more closely in a later chapter:

- **Editorial Department**: This department acquires and develops product. Acquisitions, or sponsoring, editors are responsible for one or more disciplines—that is, they research markets, sign new products, determine revision cycles for existing titles, and ensure the profitability of their disciplines. Development editors usually direct or execute the development of large-revenue packages in specific discipline areas. Editors report to a manager usually called the editorial director or editor in chief or publisher—all three terms are used in the industry for this position.

  In large companies, there quite often are several layers of management, and reporting to the editorial director are the publisher for behavioral and social sciences; the publisher for humanities; the publisher for business, etc. There may be a director of development, or development editors may report to the same manager as do acquisitions editors. In some companies, new media products are developed within the editorial department; in others, there are separate departments reporting to the editorial director or to the general manager.

- **Production and Manufacturing Departments:** The production department—usually made up of editing, art and design, and production staff—oversees print processes from final manuscript, through copy editing and design, through composition (or "typesetting"). New technologies have greatly affected the scheduling and the handling of print production stages. Some companies digitize manuscripts at the authorship stage, design and copy-edit digitized material, and send disks to printers. The manufacturing department purchases paper, printing, and binding of books and other manufacturing of non-print products, including the packaging for disks.

- **Marketing and Sales Departments:** These two groups may exist as separate departments or may report to an overall director of marketing and sales. The marketing department generally is the bridge between sales and editorial and oversees the creation of direct mail, advertising, and special promotion materials. The sales department is responsible for "representing" the company and the product on college campuses and for securing adoptions. There may also be special sales units for telemarketing, for international sales, or for sales to specialized groups such as business and government.

- **Business/ Administration/ Operations Department:** Although most college publishers have a business manager who oversees the "business" and financial aspects of that publisher, several related accounting and operations functions may be within the college publishing unit or may be part of a centralized unit for the corporation. These functions include accounts payable and accounts receivable, order entry, customer service, inventory control, and warehousing and distribution.

Stages in the Publishing Process

Later chapters will look at the publishing process in much greater detail, but for now, the process can be outlined this way:

Publishing Stage	Primary Responsibility
Market research	Acquisitions editor/ Marketing manager
Author contract	Acquisitions editor
Develop product	Development editor/ Acquisitions editor
Copy editing	Production editor
Prepress production	Production manager
Manufacturing	Production/ Manufacturing manager
Sales	Sales representative
Distribution	Warehouse/Distribution Unit

In summary:

- An acquisitions editor, sometimes working with a marketing manager, does research on a particular market segment, then seeks to put under contract the ideal author.

- The acquisitions editor, working with a development editor on larger projects, ensures that what was contracted becomes a reality—that is, confirms that it fits the market through the use of reviewers, meets the physical specifications, stays on schedule, and is profitable.

- When the "manuscript" is final, the editing, design, and production teams take over and shepherd it through to the manufacturing process.

- When the final product is in the warehouse, it is shipped to college stores to fulfill the adoptions the sales representatives have garnered.

The time from the first step to the last may be as short as six months for an electronic product and as long as seven years for a major science textbook. And a publisher may need to sink as much as $2 million into the project before realizing the first dollar from sales.

Career Paths

The people who work for college publishers generally fall into two groups: the generalists, who in their publishing careers move through a number of different kinds of jobs; and the specialists, who work their way up the career ladder within a specific area requiring professional expertise, such as accounting, design, or production. Outside of these specialized areas, almost everyone in the other positions started out as a sales representative. Today, many sales representatives choose to remain in the field for their whole careers— they really love what they're doing and love the independence with which they work. Those who do come "in house" usually first hold marketing and/or editorial positions. Almost every president of every college publishing company was a sales rep at one time.

This overview has given the realities of college publishing as illuminated by Nasrudin's streetlight. Now let's turn on the spotlight and look closely at Acquisitions and Development.

2 ACQUISITIONS & DEVELOPMENT

Let's now look inside a college publishing company to see how this industry really works. We'll begin at the beginning, when a project is first being considered by an acquisitions editor.

Acquisitions Editors

Projects are put under contract by people called acquisitions or sponsoring editors. Acquisitions editors are usually responsible for all the publications in a discipline or perhaps for several related disciplines. In some of the larger houses, a discipline may be split among several editors. For example, in the discipline of English, one person may handle publications for composition, another for literature, and a third for developmental courses. In a small house, in contrast, one editor might handle both political science and sociology.

In many ways, the acquisition editor's job is the most complex in college publishing. Several years ago the chemistry acquisitions editor at a large house decided to enroll in the MBA program at Columbia University. During an interview, his adviser asked him to describe his job as an editor. This is the job he outlined:

Acquisition Editor's Job Description

- Study the market—that is, the discipline— and from this market research, determine which courses to publish for.

- Do market research for each target course to determine what the course offerings should be. Analyze competitive course offerings.

- Determine product specifications and do financial/ profitability analysis.

- "Prospect" for the ideal author or author team.

- Successfully put the authors under contract.

- Direct or do the development of the project, including graphics and ancillaries.

- Ensure that the final product meets physical specifications, schedule, and profitability goals.

- Support marketing and sales efforts.

When the editor had finished his list, the adviser thought for a moment, then said: "You know, an MBA degree looks good on paper, but I'm not sure you need one. What you've described to me is exactly what the president of a small company does. You've already had the on-the-job-training for this degree." And some acquisitions editors are handling all these tasks on as many as twenty or even forty titles for each publication year. Now let's look a little more closely at each of these responsibilities:

Researching Markets

The first phase of market research is at the discipline level. An editor gets discipline information in a number of ways. Sales representatives are invaluable resources for giving a sense of trends, such as whether enrollments are increasing or decreasing, as well as the names of schools that are especially strong in a particular discipline. The editor also reviews catalogs from a number of different kinds of colleges and does extensive campus travel. Because the vast majority of acquisitions editors began their careers as sales representatives, the campus visiting aspect of their job is familiar and even comfortable from the beginning.

From the information gathered in all these ways, the editor may make a chart of the courses taught at freshman, sophomore, and upper levels, then plug into this chart a list of publications the publisher already has in the marketplace or under contract. Let's say the discipline is psychology. The publisher, thanks to titles inherited in a recent merger, now has six introductory texts in the marketplace and two others under contract. There are solid introductory titles for every level of rigor and perspective. So the editor looks at the next level of courses. There she finds that the enrollments in developmental psychology are very strong in child development and lifespan courses. Her publication list already has several successful titles in child development, but there is not a viable lifespan text, and she has no titles for the aging courses. Looking to junior-senior courses, she finds that there are no fresh titles for research methods, and she is convinced that one taking advantage of new technologies could capture a big chunk of the market.

Once the editor identifies the courses for which she wants to publish—in this case, a lifespan survey, a title on aging, and a multimedia research methods package—she looks even more closely at the courses, at enrollments, at what kinds of materials are being used, at what characteristics seem to be critical for success in those markets, at how many and what kinds of competitive products are in the marketplace already, and, by running a financial simulation, at whether a new entry can be profitable. She reads the journals published for that discipline to get a sense of trends and to identify major figures. Then begins the search for authors.

Prospecting for Authors

Unlike trade publishing, college publishing involves very few literary agents, so editors search for authors on their own, with the help of their sales representatives, and also with the help of authors already on their list, who know which potential authors in their discipline are in the forefront of research, for example. Also, although unsolicited manuscripts and software are considered, they rarely turn out to be appropriate for *existing* college markets. Most likely, they're old dissertations and are impenetrable—one proposal circulating a few years ago, supposedly for an economics course, was how to play the stock market based on the Book of Revelation in the Bible.

So where does the editor find ideal authors and how does she recognize them? She'll probably find them teaching at the kind of school where she expects to have the best sales for her book or disk. She'll probably learn about them from sales representatives in her company, or she may read an article by them in one of the journals of the discipline. To really be ideal, these ideal prospective authors will probably be:

- Professors who teach the course for which the product is intended.

- Professors with good academic reputations.

- For most introductory and lower-level courses, professors who are good teachers.

- Preferably professors who already have tenure, because text and new-media publishing generally don't count for much in tenure/job situations.

- Someone she'd really like to have in her life under a lot of stress for a lot of years.

What often happens is that editors from several houses identify the same potential authors, creating a competitive signing situation, which in the case of an introductory project can become quite expensive.

The money under consideration usually involves *royalties* (a set percentage of net sales), *advances* (dollars drawn against royalties, usually limited to some portion of sales expected in the first year), and *grants* (dollars given outright to authors, usually for purchase of hardware or hiring graduate assistants for research or for preparing nonsalable ancillaries). Whereas authors of "readers" may get a royalty of 8–15% of the net price, a small advance against royalties, and little or no nonreturnable grant money, a big-name academic creating an introductory package for, say, political science might get a royalty that starts at 15% of the net price and jumps up from there and an advance in the hundreds of thousands of dollars. As publishers' investments in color and ancillaries get greater, publishers often "share the risk" with authors by establishing a sliding scale for royalties that goes up as titles' sales increase above the breakeven points. Nevertheless, there have been a lot of rumors lately about the Harvard professor contracted to do an introductory economics package who got an advance against royalties said to be $1.3 million. That story even made some local newspapers. The publicity around signings like that one raises the expectations of many lesser lights writing for smaller markets and really can complicate signings.

Successful Signing

When editors find themselves in competitive signing situations, the most important piece of information they need to get is what is *really* important to the prospective author. And even when they ask directly, they don't always get a straight answer. The authors may say that quality is the most important factor, when what they really care about is money; perhaps their motivation for writing an introductory book, for example, is to put their children through college. Or it can work the other way. They may not talk about anything except money but they are really concerned about quality, or what the sales effort will be, or what will be in an ancillary package.

When editors find out what prospective authors want, the challenge is to build the case for their publishing company without *directly* putting down another company. The safest thing is to talk only about their own company and to emphasize their company's strengths. If they're from a small company, they might stress the importance of every single title to the publisher and the individual attention that authors receive. If they're from a large publisher, they might stress the sheer size and perhaps discipline specialization of the sales staff or the inhouse expertise in new media.

Let's say an editor has won a competitive signing and has contracted an author team to do the next big accounting text. What now? Well, there's an aphorism in publishing that never seems to fail. It says:

"Anything that starts badly gets worse." So the trick is to *start* well. A week spent really carefully at the beginning of a project can save weeks, months, or even years later. It's critically important for editors to let authors know exactly *what* is expected of them and *when*. Floating statements about a 2,000-page manuscript due in 36 months can lead to a lot of angst but not much else. Many editors fall back on that great truth that you can eat an elephant one bite at a time, and they start to work out a schedule with bite-size pieces. They get their authors to buy into a schedule of delivering draft chapters one at a time or in small batches, but they usually go so far as to specify how many pages a week or a month need to be produced. Getting material in small batches has several advantages: It helps authors work toward manageable goals; and it enables editors to find out early (a) if the authors can produce on schedule, and (b) if what they're producing is of acceptable quality. Establishing a careful plan for the creation of the project, then, is the first step in its development.

Development

Development of college titles is done by acquisitions editors or by development editors working under the general direction of an acquisitions editor. All projects are "developed," but the involvement of editors in this stage ranges from very slight for upper-level, specialized monographs to very intense for introductory packages with many illustrations and a large ancillary program.

Introductory packages almost always have at least one development editor, either on staff or freelance. Whereas most acquisitions editors have been sales representatives, many development editors have a background in production that has prepared them for dealing with the complexities of the large packages. Other development editors have strong academic backgrounds, and some have actually taught at the college level.

Development editors generally are specialists in broad areas such as social sciences or mathematics. Ideally they get involved at the time a project is signed—or perhaps even during the contract negotiations—and, while working closely with the acquisitions editor, they have primary responsibility for the project from first draft until it goes into production. Even after a project is in production, the acquisitions and development editors are involved in several aspects such as design.

To look more closely at this process, let's track the development of an introductory biology text. With all the new media around, text**books** are—at least this week—still the primary platform for delivery of educational materials.

During development, editors are looking for what is innovative about a project, what will make it stand out from the crowd, but editors keep five overriding questions in mind:

Primary Development Criteria

- Does the project fit the course? Faculty are not going to create a new course or create a new way to teach just because one of the twenty-five new books in any given year is different.

- Is it comprehensive? Especially at the introductory level, texts are expected to be a compendium of the generally accepted content of that discipline.

- Is it accurate? At the introductory level there should be few opinions and many facts, and the facts must be right.

- Is it up to date? Electronic media have led all of us to want current information, but it is critical in many disciplines.

- Is it accessible? Can the students at the target schools handle the vocabulary, for example, and is the material presented in a way that will interest them?

With these criteria, development begins. The usual stages in development are:
- Development plan
- First draft
- Review
- Second draft
- Review
- Final draft(s)

Although this looks like a neat list, some chapters may go through four or even six drafts. Complicating everything is the art program, which for an introductory biology package is extraordinarily difficult to create. Let's look more closely at these stages:

Development Plan

Book specifications:

    1,200 pages

    8 1/2 x 11" trim size

    5-color throughout

Art specifications/budget:

    600 4-color photographs/research: $130,000

    500 line drawings: $92,000

Schedule

    Contract signed: 2/1/93

    First draft complete: 2/1/96

    Second draft text, first draft art complete: 2/1/97

    Revised draft complete: 12/1/97

    To production: 3/1/98

    Bound books: 9/1/99

Ancillary plan

Book Specifications

A first important kind of planning involves the physical specifications of the book. Because the acquisitions editor has studied the way this course is taught, he knows that to fit the introductory market, the book should be about 1,200 pages long, broken into chapters that fit the two-semester or three-quarter course.

In considering the trim size, the editor knows that a two-column design will help control length and give the greatest flexibility in sizing and placing the very large art program and that he needs to go to 8 1/2 x 11" —a relatively expensive size—in order to have a two-column book but also an open and inviting page.

The book must be four-color throughout to accommodate the anticipated 600 color photographs. One problem with four-, or process-, color, however, is that the colors needed for printing are black, yellow, a rather pale blue, and a pinkish red—all virtually useless, or too ugly, for any other applications such as colored subheads or tints. So this editor goes for the expense of a fifth color so that he can use a handsome green in heads and other design elements of the book.

Art Specifications & Budget

To be pedagogically effective, biology books must be heavily illustrated, with a number of different kinds of illustrations (art for other disciplines can be considerably less expensive than the specialized art needed for biology). Many of the photographs of things like trees, flowers, and animals can be obtained from photo agents at a cost of $75–225 each for use at a quarter-page size for one-time North American reproduction rights. Going to a half page doubles the cost of the rights; going to world reproduction rights is also double whatever the size cost is. For the anticipated 600 color photographs and the photo research costs for obtaining rights, the editor estimates that the cost will be approximately $130,000.

Biology books also must illustrate clearly human and plant anatomy and physiology, as well as other structures. Specially trained illustrators must be found to execute many of these illustrations, which go through an extensive drafting and reviewing process. The cost for the estimated 500 illustrations will be about $92,000.

Cost: Thus, the estimate for obtaining the necessary illustrations for this introductory biology book is more than $220,000; the production and manufacturing costs will be on top of this.

Schedule

Professors of biology, like most of the sciences with lab courses, do not like to change texts any more often than they have to, which usually means only when there's a new edition of their current text. Thus, it's critically important that this new text be published the year that its major competitor is going into a new edition. In this case, the two texts that this one is targeted to compete with most directly are scheduled for new editions on January 1 of the year 2000. This means that these competitors will be brought out in the fall of 1999 so that sales representatives can begin preselling from the books themselves. Thus, the bound-book date of this new book *and its ancillaries*—September 1999—is on a do-or-die schedule. If the book does not come out then, it probably will not get another chance at adoptions until 2003, when it will be out of date. To meet that schedule, here's when the major steps must be completed:

> Contract signed: 2/1/93
>
> First draft complete: 2/1/96
>
> Second-draft text, first-draft art complete: 12/1/97
>
> To production: 3/1/98
>
> Bound books: 9/1/99

Notice that for the first edition of a large, color book, 18 months *may* be needed from final manuscript to bound books, though for projects less complex than biology, 12 months is closer to average. (Chapter 3 will discuss the details of production and manufacturing that can make this process so lengthy for complex projects.)

Ancillary Plan

Although ancillary plans will not be finalized until a project is well under way, it's important that the editor come up with a fairly accurate list so that they can be budgeted. Also, the schedule planning for ancillaries is critical. If they are not ready with the book, sales can be seriously affected. In this case, the free materials for instructors include an instructor's manual, print and computerized tests, a color overhead/slide set; and a videodisk. Materials for sale to students include a study guide and computerized study guide; a lab manual with computer simulation; and a CD-I, an interactive program. As the project develops, the editor will make decisions about what the content will be for the videodisk, lab simulation, and CD-I.

Cost: The editor budgets $600,000 for acquisition and production—but not manufacturing—of these ancillaries.

Drafts & Reviews

As the manuscript comes in, the development editor carefully monitors it for the characteristics mentioned above—fit with course, comprehensiveness, accuracy, timeliness, and accessibility. In many ways, the development editor himself or herself takes responsibility for the accessibility by assuming the role of surrogate student and may extensively rewrite the material.

For the other criteria, editors rely very heavily on reviewers, and for introductory packages they use two kinds of reviewers: specialists, who do so-called development reviews of chapters in their special area of expertise; and generalists, people who teach the course for which the book is intended, the best of whom will review all chapters in all drafts. The specialist reviewers may not actually teach the course—they are more likely involved in research and in teaching upper-level courses such as microbiology. Their special contribution is to ensure that individual chapters in their area are accurate and up to date, with the most recent research findings; they probably also review the graphics for their chapters.

The specialists usually review first and second drafts; generalists review all drafts, including a fairly large number doing "marketing reviews" of the final draft—relatively fast and short reviews that give a final check that the book in fact fits its market.

When the first manuscript comes in, the development editor may send it out for review or may critique it and have the author make revisions before the first draft goes out to reviewers. When first-draft reviews come in, the development editor collates comments and gives the author recommendations about how to revise; the editor may also do line editing at this stage, incorporating reviewers' comments. The interpretations are very important; an editor can almost never simply send reviews to authors. In the first place, they almost never agree with each other, so the editor needs to give some direction about which comments to follow. One way the reviews tend to disagree is on what's included—or more accurately, what's left out. What the specialists usually want to add is material from their research that would raise the level of the book up somewhere near the postdoctoral level. Everyone —specialists and generalists—has his or her pet subjects, and if you put in everything everyone wants, you'd have a 3,000-page book. The perfect cube. You'd have to give training wheels with each copy.

The second-draft reviews are especially a valuable check on accuracy, to see that in revising the first draft no errors of fact or emphasis crept in. There may also be a review stage after the third, or final, draft for the same purpose.

One interesting aspect of reviewing is when and why reviews take place, compared to trade books. Texts are reviewed in progress to ensure that they are right for the course. Trade books are reviewed after publication to let readers know whether or not they want to buy a book. As was noted earlier, no professor would adopt a core textbook for classroom use on the basis of a review, even if it were in the most prestigious journal of the discipline.

Cost: For the first edition of an introductory biology text, editors may use as many as twenty-five specialist reviewers, a dozen whole-book generalist reviewers, and fifty marketing reviewers. The budget for reviewing a text like this may be as much as $200,000. For texts in other disciplines and at higher levels, the number of reviewers needed and the cost of the reviews may be a small fraction of this amount.

Although design is considered part of "production," a book such as an introductory biology text is usually designed during development, because the design can determine how some elements—such as set-off boxes—need to be written, and typeface for the labels on illustrations must be determined very early in the process.

Overall, then, development consists of reviewing and revising successive drafts until a final draft that meets the quality and discipline-needs criteria is ready for production along with a clearly planned, if not finally executed, art program, while at the same time controlling budget and schedule for that stage of the project. As was noted, for the first edition of a complex package like this one, the time for development can easily be five years, or longer, and the cost more than a million dollars. On the other hand, the development time for a second-course computer science text, if it is done in print, may be just a matter of months.

Nonprint Products

This discussion of acquisitions and development so far has tracked the progress of a book. But what if the product is nonprint?

All the first stages for the acquisitions editor in terms of market research, seeking an author, and negotiating a contract are very similar. A big difference for products other than large-course surveys—a CD-ROM, for example, that is intended to be used as a *supplement* in a world history course—is that the electronic product may be finished before the editor sees it or negotiates the contract.

If the decision for the introduction to biology is to do a multimedia product instead of a book, some of the stages are the same, some of the processes different.

Fairly early on, the developers begin to story-board screens based on the curriculum to access the content. For ancillary products, the developers may begin with story-boarded screens, from which they develop content.

For the content itself, the same stages of drafts, reviews, and revisions are followed. However, early on, the development group also involves a technical team, and this shift affects how the art program is developed, as videos and animations are added to the mix. It also, in the end, affects how the "text" itself is handled.

At the end, besides content reviews, there also have to be technical reviews to ensure that the whole product is "user friendly." Many of the costs for developing an electronic product are about the same as for the equivalent stages in print—things like author advances and grants, reviewing, copy editing—while others are much higher—such as product design or permissions to reproduce (if rights are available at all).

One major difference is that many aspects of production are done during development for electronic product, so the eighteen months needed for production and manufacturing for the biology survey is dramatically reduced. The time and cost for duplicating a CD-ROM is considerably less than for printing and binding a 1,200-page four-color book. But for now, so is the size of the market for wholly electronic product.

Conclusion

In summary, then, editors are much like the conductors of an orchestra: After they decide which piece is both appropriate for their audience and playable by their ensemble, they orchestrate the playing of the whole piece. They don't have to be able to play each instrument, but they sure better know when to bring each one in, and they have to ensure that the violins and the horns are playing the same tempo.

3 PRODUCTION & MANUFACTURING

A story from a number of years ago tells a classic tale of a production and manufacturing person's worst nightmare, while also illustrating some key stages in these processes. The project was an introductory psychology textbook—in fact, the first college text ever created using full color throughout.

The story really began when the final manuscript was sent to a copy editor, who was asked, in addition to styling the manuscript, to suggest places where the available color could be used pedagogically. When the copy editor was working on the chapter on senses and perception, she encountered the statement that color-blind people do not experience a total lack of color. Some people are green-red "blind" and tend to experience an absence of those colors while others are blue-yellow–blind; very few see the world only in gray tones. She suggested that showing the gradations of color blindness would be a fine, pedagogical, nongimmicky way to use color.

The art director hired a photographer to go out and shoot pictures of Union Square in San Francisco—which at that time was a richly colored scene, with green grass and trees, colorful cable cars, and brightly dressed people eating lunch on the benches. The art director and production manager then worked closely with consultants who were vision specialists and the company doing the color separations in preparation for printing. They were very careful to create a two-page spread—kind of a photo essay on color vision—that showed the scene the way someone with "normal" color vision saw it but also the way people with red-green, blue-yellow, and monochromatic vision saw it. The consultants confirmed that the illustrations were accurate and praised the pedagogical soundness of showing a phenomenon that had not been previously illustrated in a college textbook.

Well, you can imagine what the marketing folks did with that one. The word went out to campuses across the country that instructors could finally show their students—at least the ones with normal vision—what color blindness looked like.

When the time came for the book to be printed, the art director and the production/manufacturing director flew to the Midwest, where the book was being printed, to check this first full-color book on press. The actual printing would take place over a period of several days. All was going well until late the night of the second day. The art director and production/manufacturing director had come back from dinner and were lounging in the press room, feeling quite satisfied about the fine quality of the printing and the large meal they had just eaten.

Suddenly, they heard a shout from one of the press operators who was checking sheets coming off press: "Good grief! Would you look at that! How in the hell did this happen? Hey, Joe, run up the red—run it way up. Run up the yellow. This color is really lousy!"

When the publishers went over to look at the problem—you guessed it—it was the color-blindness spread that had upset the press operator so much. Had the publishers lingered over dinner much longer, perhaps had dessert, all the careful work done during the production stages would have been negated during printing.

If the press operator's "color correcting" had continued, there would have been a disaster for the publisher. The publisher had to get this color right, because it was in a sense proving to the industry that there were sound pedagogical reasons for using color. Because the schedule was so tight and the print run was so large, using so much specially manufactured paper, there probably would have been no way to reprint those pages and still have the book ready for that narrow window of time when adoption decisions are made. But the story had a happy ending, which in many ways changed the way introductory college textbooks have looked ever since.

At the time this story took place—and for a long time before and after—the production and manufacturing processes could be laid out in a neat, linear flowchart. A few things, like the preparation of the cover and the index, might be on a branch off to the side, but mostly the processes flowed in an orderly way.

Today, because of some of the new digital production and manufacturing technologies being used, it is impossible to diagram all the ways the processes happen without a hologram. For this discussion, we'll begin with that basic chart, then consider some of its variations. In fact, the great majority of books still follow this model. After looking at books, we'll turn to some of the variations that come up for nonprint products.

Here, then, are the usual stages in the production and manufacturing of a print product, each one of which we'll look at in some depth:

Production/Manufacturing Flowchart

Final Manuscript to Production
Interior Design
Copy Editing
Author Review
Composition
First Proofs/Proofreading
Jacket/Cover Design
Second Proofs/Proofreading
Indexing
Prepress
Manufacturing

Final Manuscript to Production

In most publishing houses, the final manuscript is officially transmitted from the editorial department to the production department at a launch, or transmittal, meeting. Even if the product is electronic, there is usually a manuscript of its text. Also, although a print product may be handled in digitized form through production, the disk is most often accompanied by a printout.

The launch meeting is usually attended by the acquisitions and development editors, the production team, and also the marketing manager, who gets valuable early information about the product and contributes ideas for elements like the cover. The production team usually consists of a production editor, who reports to the managing editor; a designer/art director, who reports to the director of art and design; and a production manager, who reports to the head of production and manufacturing.

The launch meeting typically begins with a very brief presentation by the acquisitions editor or development editor, focusing on the level of and market for the book, so that the production team will have a sense of the course level, design complexity, and "look" that is wanted. The final manuscript—in theory, if not always in fact— consists of complete text, complete captions, complete reference material for illustrations, complete labels for illustrations, complete permissions cleared, even complete preface and table of contents. In fact, there often is some material missing—perhaps permissions have been requested but all have not come in. Also, for large, complex projects, the design and illustration program may have been begun earlier. But in general, this is the opportunity for each member of the production team to get the answers they need in order to do their jobs. Here's what each is responsible for:

Production Team Assignments

Production Editor: The production editor surveys the manuscript to ensure that it is complete and to prepare it for copy editing and design. For copy editing, the production editor prepares a preliminary style sheet, outlining how specific style points should be handled and how subheads and other design elements should be marked, and directing the copy editor to perform any other tasks that may be needed, such as verifying that citations for quotations are properly handled. For design, the production editor prepares a memo with samples of every element in the manuscript that needs to be designed. This design memo might include, for example, the longest and shortest chapter titles so that the designer can accommodate both. If photo research is needed but was not handled during development, the production editor or art director hires or assigns that specialist. These steps take place no matter what the medium of the product.

Designer/Art Director: The art director is responsible for determining the design needs for the book, including text, illustrations, and cover. In most companies, the art director hires freelance designers and illustrators. This way, there is flexibility in matching a designer's "look" with the needs of the project. For example, an art director might choose one designer for an introductory literature anthology where the design needs to be "classy" but open for weaker students, but choose a different designer for an upper-level, financial accounting text, where clear treatment of tabular material is critical. The art director also at this stage estimates all the costs incurred in the art and design work. This model is essentially the same for print and nonprint products.

Production Manager: As part of the author-contract negotiations, a preliminary schedule and cost estimate were prepared. But several or even many years may have passed since they were done, and many aspects of the project may have changed. Increasingly during this period of technological transition, new media are being added to packages, and products are being published in multiple formats—all of which adds to the cost of startup, especially since the electronic files often must be prepared in several formats.

In almost every case, production and manufacturing prices will have risen since that initial estimate. So the first important step for the production manager is to prepare a new estimate based on the current specifications for the project. This preparation involves going to several vendors who can do this kind of project—and they are specialized not only for medium but for size and literally shape of the project—and getting competitive bids and schedules. When the production manager receives this information, he or she puts it together with the production editor's and art director's estimates to come up with a total production and manufacturing estimate and a schedule. Again, this model is the same for print and nonprint products.

At this point, the acquisitions editor takes a hard look at the new cost estimates relative to the pricing of the project to ensure that it is still profitable. If it is not, alternatives must be considered. One possibility is to not publish, but that is an unlikely choice for a project that has come this far. For books, it is more likely that some of the physical specifications will be changed. Perhaps the manuscript will be shortened; perhaps less color or fewer illustrations will be used; or perhaps the book will be designed to be printed in a more economical trim size. The physical book—if the product is a book—has enormous impact on the profitability. The things that affect the cost of a single unit— variables such as size and color—can make or break the bottom line, because this cost is incurred for every copy printed, whether it's sold, given away, or—God forbid—left sitting in the warehouse.

While the production manager is getting these estimates, the design and copy editing are usually begun.

Interior Design

Designing for the college market has one special challenge: not only does the interior design have to be attractive but it also has to function pedagogically for its intended market. Let's look at just a few of the many elements that must be considered. Again, we'll primarily consider print products, though there are analogous elements for electronic products.

Key Design Elements

> Typeface
> Type Size
> Column Width
> Treatment of Heads
> Treatment of Folios/Running Heads

Typeface: The look of the typeface tells a lot about the "attitude" of a project. A sans serif typeface tends to look more modern than a face with a serif; for example, consider two frequently used faces, Helvetica and Century Schoolbook, both set in the same size:

This is Helvetica, a frequently used sans serif typeface.

This is Century Schoolbook, a frequently used serif typeface.

You can notice several things besides the presence or absence of the short lines, or serifs, on the individual letters. Helvetica seems more modern. Century Schoolbook looks somewhat larger.

It is more likely that a face like Helvetica would be chosen for a modern art project than, say, a history of Greece. Because many people—especially older people—seem to find serif faces easier to read, they are usually chosen for wordy texts like anthologies. Interestingly, studies have shown that young people can read sans serif as easily as serif—possibly because they are so used to seeing it in advertising—but once again, it's the professor, with "older eyes," who chooses a book, and professors can accept or reject a book on the basis of this kind of look even though they may not be conscious of why they like or don't like it.

Type Size: Type size affects both look and readability. If there is a length problem, a designer would probably choose a typeface that sets smaller than Century Schoolbook. There are hundreds of faces, and the sizes can be controlled digitally so that a designer can use a slightly smaller typeface with increased space above and below the type to save space and still have readable type.

Column Width: A major decision is whether type will run in one or two columns. Students tend to prefer the look of a single column—it seems more open and inviting—but it has its disadvantages. For one, the human eye seems to be able to track from the end of one line to the beginning of the next only if the line is relatively short. How short depends upon the size of the type. Today's students, who are not especially good readers, cannot easily read a book if the text line width exceeds about 5 inches. What happens is that they find the text hard, when in fact it's the design rather than the content that causes the difficulty. A great deal more readable words fit on a page with two columns, and a two-column design also gives considerable flexibility in the size of illustrations. So a relatively short literature anthology in a smallish trim size will probably be single column, but an introductory text that is heavily illustrated will often be in a large trim size so that an open-looking two-column format can be used.

Treatment of Heads: The most important pedagogical concern for heads is that the heads stand out clearly and that levels of subheading are obvious. Especially when heads are placed in the margin, head structure can effectively function as an outline of the material, which helps a student master it.

Treatment of Folios/Running Heads: How the folios, or page numbers, are handled can be a critical element in some books. Think about a really classy design, where the folios are always flushed right. That design could be very effective for a novel. But if the work is a reference book, the page numbers on all lefthand pages would be in the gutter, where they can't easily be seen. Similarly, running heads help students know where they are. The best designs for reference-type works often put the running head, the folio, and any letter keys used in cross referencing all together in the outside margin at the top or bottom of the page.

As you can see, literally, elements of design for the college market are complex, often subtle, and critically important. When page makeup is done, the sizing and positioning of illustrations are other critical aspects of design. New electronic technologies—whether used for print or for nonprint products—now give designers great flexibility as well as relative ease in doing makeup, and products have significantly improved pedagogically for that reason.

Costs: For freelance designers, one-time four-color design costs run about $2,000–3,500 for an introductory text.

Copy Editing

The hidden heroes of the publishing process are the copy editors. They are the last editors to work on an entire project before it is manufactured. The usual description of their role is to impose consistent spelling and grammatical usage, to code design elements such as heads and set-off material for the designer, and sometimes to check facts or to smooth out the language. What does not come out of those phrases clearly is that they also save publishers from embarrassment at the least and, occasionally, from lawsuits at worst.

These specialists are almost always freelances—again, in college publishing, where most projects are on the same schedule, a publisher might need fifty or sixty copy editors at one time of year and five or six at another. And an uncanny number turn out to be Virgos.

Increasingly, copy editors work on computers, handling many of the keyboarding and online editing tasks that used to be done by compositors. One problem when copy editors work on computers is determining how to let authors review the editing. There are tracer programs so that authors can see material underlined or stricken through when there are changes, but these programs work best, as does editing on screen, when the project is not a technical or mathematical one with, for example, built up fractions.

Costs: Copy editors average 100+ manuscript pages per week—and as many as 200 pages per week if there is much reprint material, as for anthologies. The usual rate for copy editing is $15–25 dollars per hour, depending upon experience and specialization, and the total cost for a complex 1,000–page book (about a 2,500-page manuscript) would be between $8,000 and $12,000.

Author Review

Authors almost always review copy-edited manuscript (1) to respond to queries and requests from the copy editor and (2) to ensure that meaning has not been changed during the copy editing. For first-time authors, the initial encounter with a copy-edited manuscript aflutter with Post-Its usually provokes despair or rage—or both, when the queries say things like: "Please confirm the dates here. Was he 117 years old when he was inaugurated?" By the time the authors have gone through the manuscript, they sometimes—but not always—are so filled with gratitude that their reputations have been preserved that they add the copy editor's name to the list of acknowledgments.

Composition

Composition, or typesetting, is one area of production that has been so greatly affected by new technologies that, to survive at all, compositors are dramatically changing the services they offer. What compositors have always done is to set type. At first they set individual letters, then single lines of type.

When computers first started being used by compositors, in the early 1970s, the vocabulary started to change. They talked about a two-stage process of capturing keystrokes, then outputting them in reproducible form. As publishers and authors began to use word processors and computers, it was they—not the compositors—who captured the keystrokes. In those early days, there were three big problem areas: First, there were about as many kinds of computers and software as there were authors, and they were not necessarily compatible with the compositors' computers and typesetting equipment. A big question of compositors was what software translation programs could be used effectively. One of the best, York Graphic Services, offered more than 80 conversion programs back then.

A second problem area was copy editing: Who would insert the copy-editing changes into the disk? If compositors did so, they charged as if it were a correction cycle, and it often turned out to be cheaper to let the author work on a computer but to send the compositor a copy-edited manuscript.

The third problem, similar to the second, was how to imbed design codes into the disk. Few authors or copy editors had the skill to do this, and compositors charged for it as they would for making corrections in a proof stage.

As computers, software, and people became more sophisticated, publishers were able to supply copy-edited, design-keyed disks for books that were straight text. As desktop scanners and page-building software were developed, some publishers reached the stage of being able to do their own page make-up. The whole process of composition—whether for a print or for a nonprint product— effectively moved inhouse at many publishing companies and moved partially inhouse at others. When people talk about desktop publishing at a publishing company, this is what they usually mean: being able to bring inhouse the composition and makeup processes and have them produced by specially trained editors and designers.

The best of the compositors have shifted their business in accordance with technological changes in order to complement publishers' inhouse systems. They still offer fairly straightforward composition for those who want it, but they have really beefed up their electronic prepress services, as we'll discuss below.

The major trends in composition have included developing standard coding such as the Standard Generalized Markup Language, or SGML, so that one editorial data base can be created and can be manipulated for both paper and electronic media in many different formats. SGML is being used by businesses and governmental agencies internationally, but it also has had some interesting impact in educational publishing, especially at the elementary and high school levels. The State of Texas, for example, requires that all educational material adopted for its schools be available with SGML so that the electronic files can be used to create Braille, large-print, and synthesized-voice versions of textbooks for use by print-disabled people.

Costs: Total composition costs might run from $30,000 on a simple, one-color book to more than $300,000 for a four-color accounting text. The average composition cost for ancillaries—many of which are done by desktop methods—is about $3,000 each.

First Proofs & Proofreading

In traditional publishing, the first stage of proofs is called galley proofs—an archaic term going back to the days when Linotypes, hot-metal machines, set one line of type at a time. Galleys were the metal trays that held these unpaginated lines of type.

Today, if a compositor keyboards a manuscript, the output may be roughly broken into pages but probably will not have page numbers or artwork in place. Proofreaders—again, freelances—read first proof against the manuscript from which it was set, looking for typographical errors and omitted material, as well as any inconsistencies or errors that a copy editor may have missed. The cost for proofreading, very roughly, is about half what it is for copy editing.

If the publisher is working in digitized form and supplying a disk to the compositor, the "final manuscript" is the equivalent of the first proof. Thus, in many ways, the copy editor is also a proofreader. If a publisher supplies a disk, the first proof may be equivalent to the second proof of a more traditional process.

At this point in the cycle, the cover design is usually being done.

Jacket & Cover Design

Perhaps you really can't judge a book by its cover, but a lot of people do, including professors facing a stack of examination copies on their desk. Some of the same subtleties that mark interior design also are true for the cover or jacket design (jackets are the paper dust jackets found most commonly on hardback trade books). Just as a sans serif typeface in the interior design communicates that this is a "modern" book, so does the use of that kind of type on the cover.

The first factor affecting cover design is the physical specifications of the book. Is it paperback or is it hard cover? If it is paperback, it will have a cover. If it is hard cover, it may have a colorful preprinted cover, or it may have a relatively plain "cloth" cover and a dustjacket. Also, what is the trim size? If it's a small book with a long title and several authors, there may not be room for anything except type on the cover.

How many colors are available? Will the cover be one-color or two-color or four-color? Will there be only type or will there be a photograph or an illustration?

These questions begin to address the critical issue of what the cover must communicate. Consider some of the possibilities, for example, for a political science text. A cover that has only the author's name and the book's title in a conservative typeface makes a very different impression than one that has a color photograph of the American flag or one that has a naive painting of the

Revolutionary War or one that has a Herblock cartoon. The all-type cover may communicate that this is a serious, scholarly work—probably inappropriate for a low-level institution—whereas the cartoon may signal an inviting book but one that possibly has an inherent political bias.

Because the cover design needs are so diverse, publishers almost entirely use freelance designers whose particular styles fit the image wanted for a book. Some designers are exceptionally talented at creating all-type designs; others tend to use only works of abstract art on covers; while still others favor photographs. Often the cover designer for an introductory text also designs covers for other major elements of the package.

Costs: A four-color cover design could cost $1,500–2,500 plus permissions costs for any artwork used; one- and two-color cover designs are usually somewhat cheaper. If a designer or design studio is doing the interior and cover designs for a package, the cost can run about $15,000 plus cost of art permissions. If they are also laying out, or dummying, the text, that figure would be much higher.

Second Proofs/Proofreading

The second proofs—or perhaps the first, if a disk was provided—are usually made-up pages, with at least low-resolution scans of artwork in place. In most instances publishers are working at this stage with a compositor, but a number of freelance design services now exist that can handle made-up pages on even the most complex books.

Proofreading at this stage usually includes, first, reading to catch any typographical or factual errors that may have crept in; and, second, checking the makeup itself. How does the page look? Are running heads and folios correct and in place? Are any equations or complex material broken up by page breaks? Is artwork the correct size and positioned close to its text reference? Is the artwork right-side up? These are the kinds of questions a proofreader at this stage considers, no matter what the eventual medium.

Indexing

Preparation of the table of contents and index can be done after page proofs are made up. There are now excellent software programs that can make up tables of contents from electronically tagged heads and subheads and can make up indexes from electronically tagged words in the text.

These are, however, two instances where even though you can do something, you may not want to. If the book has a relatively simple table of contents with few subheads, it might be easier just to keyboard it from page proofs than to embed electronic tabs. Similarly, there are limitations to indexing software that may make it better to do an index manually. These limitations are the inability of a program to cross-reference automatically and the inability of a program to index a concept when the exact term for the concept is not used.

Costs: Professional indexers charge, on average, a dollar per line/entry. Thus, a full index for a complex, introductory text could run $5,000–8,000.

Prepress

Prepress is a catchall term that could include all the production stages outlined above but most generally refers to those steps that physically convert text and images into a form that can be used to manufacture the product.

Let's consider print first. Text and images need to be prepared in a way so that their impression is made upon paper. Again, we'll begin with a greatly simplified description of what is older technology, because many printed products still go through this process.

Prepress Stages
Capture text
Capture, separate, and screen images
Make composite film or disk

Text: First, in the more traditional process, captured text is run through a processor that generates "galleys"—there's that word again— of type in film. The text film galleys will be assembled by hand with the illustrations, following a page-by-page layout or a comprehensive set of page–make-up specifications provided by the publisher.

Images: In a separate process, photographs—that is, continuous-tone images—are given very special handling. Continuous-tone images cannot print as they are—they would just make black blobs.

In order to be printed, these images themselves must be photographed through a fine screen. This screen creates on the film dots of varying density that show the details of the original tones from gray to black; it is these dots that will ultimately print the screened images, known as halftones. The image film is used for page assembly with the text film. All of this assembly is known as stripping.

For color, such as color photographs, presses use four so-called process-color inks—cyan (blue), magenta (red), yellow, and black—to create the full spectrum of colors we see on a printed page. For a halftone in color, scanners separate the image, generating four pieces of film, in preparation for four-color-process printing. Once again, multiple pieces of film for the text, photos, and art are stripped to create final composite film pages.

Costs: For a 1,200–page biology text, the cost of shooting and stripping text would be about $70,000; for illustrations, about $115,000, for a total of about $185,000.

Film: Most page stripping is done using positive film—that is, the light and dark areas correspond to the final printed page. The positive film is then contacted to other film to produce negative film for the printer. With the exception of digital printing and some on-demand printing methods, nearly all printers make textbook printing plates from page negatives. The negative areas hold the ink to print positively on paper.

New technologies have greatly affected many of these processes. Both black-and-white and color images can now be scanned digitally and the digital images put in place with the digital type, for example. Printing plates can often be made directly from the digital material, eliminating the film stages for one-color and less-complex jobs. As these technologies have evolved, vendors who do prepress work have spent literally millions of dollars on developing hardware and software. Although the processes may appear to be simpler and easier, in fact they require an enormous investment in research and development, in equipment, and in training the people who use them, which has limited the number of vendors who fully can take advantage of them.

Nonprint Production

How then does the production of electronic products differ? The first big difference is that publishers know in advance that they are developing an electronic product and they take advantage of new technologies from the beginning. In a sense, production itself is part of development. Text and images are created or scanned in a form so that they can be manipulated and repurposed throughout the process; the development essentially takes place in the medium of the final product. As we noted above, the team for electronic product includes some new members— technical specialists, as well as curriculum design experts. If the electronic product is to be interactive, programmers are critical. Some of the largest compositors have adapted their businesses to be able to handle production of multimedia, both as original products and as "repurposed" products.

Costs: It is instructive to compare the development and production costs and schedules of (A) a 1,200-page introductory text; (B) the same text and graphics also spun off unchanged (dumped) in an alternative electronic format, an unlikely but possible event; and (C) a separately developed electronic product with equivalent discipline coverage. The numbers are very rough but are comparable with each other:

Book and CD-ROM Development/Production

Product/Stage	Cost	Time
A. *Book devel./prod.*	$750,000	48 mos.
B. *Spinoff disk* *devel./prod.*	0	6 wks
C. *Electronic* *devel./prod.*	$600,000	36 mos

As you can see, development and production costs for a book total about $750,000, with a total time of approximately 48 months. If an alternate, electronic version of the same text and graphics were spun off, the total additional cost and time would be negligible. For a wholly electronic *equivalent* product, the cost for development would be approximately the same, but production costs would be relatively minimal. The development time would be about the same, but the production time would be short because so much "production" occurs during development of electronic product. When we look at manufacturing, we'll compare the unit costs of these same products.

Manufacturing

Manufacturing departments—or the production manager, if manufacturing is not centralized—have traditionally been responsible for purchasing paper, printing, and binding, or PP&B. For the most part, they still are. They also now purchase the manufacturing and packaging of electronic products. Again, let's look at print products first.

Print Manufacturing Purchases

Paper: Several considerations must be made regarding paper. The first, *size*, is a function of the trim size of a book. Papers are manufactured in fairly standard sheet and roll sizes that fit the most frequently used presses.

For college publishing, the most common sizes are 6 x 9", 7 1/2 x 9 1/4", 8 x 10", and 8 1/2 x 11". Other sizes are less economical; usually one of these standard sizes must be used and trimmed down, with paper waste, for other sizes. Another factor is *opacity*, how much show-through there is. Opacity is related to the weight and coating of a paper. For very large tomes, publishers might like to use a "Bible stock," but if the large tome is a literature anthology, where students tend to use highlighters, a very thin paper would be problematic.

Paper overall is the largest single cost factor on books, easily 60 to 80 percent of the unit PP&B cost. Huge increases in paper costs in recent years—as much as 50%—have really put stress on publishers' margins, because they simply don't have the pricing flexibility to pass on all of these cost increases.

Printing: Different printers have different kinds of printing equipment, and publishers choose the printers who can most effectively and economically print the size and the quantity needed. For a small-quantity, high-quality black-and-white photography book, a production manager might select a printer who has presses that print single sheets relatively slowly. For an introductory accounting text whose print run is 100,000 copies, the production or manufacturing manager would choose a printer who has a high-speed, four-color web press that can print 17,000 to 22,000 32-page signatures an hour. Paper spoilage is high with fast presses, so the kind of press chosen for the accounting book probably would not be used for a printing smaller than 15,000 copies. It would waste as much paper to print 1,000 copies as to print 100,000 copies on that press.

There are a number of interesting trends in printing, both taking advantage of new technologies and meeting changing market needs. Among the new technologies, presses are being developed that print directly from digitized data, and many smaller-quantity presses using new technologies are emerging to meet needs for customized product and printing on demand. Customized product and printing on demand have created some serious challenges for both publishers and college stores. The stores that have installed their own DocuTech equipment have suffered through the expensive startup phases of this technology right along with the publishers.

Binding: Sheets that come off press are folded, either in a separate operation or on the printing line of web presses, into signatures most commonly of 32 pages. On the binding line, these signatures are collated and bound, and the cover is attached.

Very generally, there are two kinds of binding: adhesives and sewing. There have been great improvements in adhesives in recent years, and adhesive bindings are the most common for both hardcover and paperback books. It's certainly possible for there to be a glitch so that a single book has a binding flaw, but if there is a problem, it is more likely that a fairly large number of books are involved and the person at fault is none other than Mother Nature. When books come off the binding line and then are exposed either in the warehouse or more likely during transit to extremes of humidity or temperature, the adhesives may be affected. To meet that adoption window of opportunity, many books are printed in midwinter, and most of the time when bindings give way, the books have sat overnight in a truck or a freight car in subzero temperatures.

The other kind of binding, sewing, is exactly what it sounds like. A huge sewing machine stitches the signatures together. This process is very slow and expensive, and it tends to be used only for reference-type books that get heavy use and where its characteristic of opening flat is a special advantage. (Parenthetically, in contrast to college publishing, elementary and high school books must adhere to a strict—and expensive—set of binding requirements and cover materials so that they "can't" fall apart during the number of years for which they're adopted.)

Electronic Product

Manufacture of electronic product usually consists of giving the manufacturer a master of the product and the packaging for the duplicates. In comparison to the manufacture of a book, it's fast and relatively inexpensive.

Costs: As we did for developmental and production costs, let's compare the manufacturing costs for equivalent print and nonprint products.

Book and CD-ROM Manufacturing

Product/Stage	Unit Cost	Time
A. *Book PP&B*	$8.00	6 weeks
B. *CD-ROM mfg.*	$1.50	1 week

As we noted in the Introduction, the current potential of technology far exceeds its use. Although no publisher is sure what the platform for products will be a few years from now, it's clear from our examination of production and manufacturing that publishers, as the content providers, face the trend toward electronic product with great optimism, if for no other reason than that production and manufacturing costs will be greatly reduced. But in fact these new electronic products offer such great flexibility in teaching and in learning that, as a creative industry, publishers especially look forward to that aspect too.

4 MARKETING & SALES

Once a book comes off press, marketing and sales people work to meet their most important task: they must get the right book or disk into the hands of a potential adopter at the right time—that narrow window when adoptions are made, because no professor will adopt for course work a product she or he has not seen. That's why publishers spend such a large proportion of their net sales dollars—between 15 and 20 percent, on average, or about $163 million dollars as an industry—on marketing and sales. So how *do* the right products get to the right people?

Well, there's one story about the chair of the humanities department at a state college who controlled all the adoptions in humanities but refused to see any sales representatives. An energetic new sales rep peeked into his office one day and saw that his walls were plastered with posters from France. The next day the rep barged into his office at noon with a blue-checked tablecloth and a basket laden with roast chicken, cheese, bread, and wine, and she began speaking to him in French. She got the adoptions . . . in French, introduction to humanities, and art appreciation.

Fortunately, most reps don't have to be French-speaking chefs to qualify for their job. But they do need this kind of persistence and imagination to make contact with faculty and be sure that they get the right books or disks to them, and also that their products get a fair examination. In this chapter, we'll see how the marketing and sales people work together to ensure just that.

Marketing and sales responsibilities may be handled by a single department or by two separate departments or by separate staffs reporting to one department head, probably the most usual structure. No two publishers have exactly the same internal structure for marketing and sales, but the major *functional* areas can be outlined:

Marketing and Sales Department Staffs

VP of Sales and Marketing
    Director of Marketing
        Marketing Managers
        Advertising Manager
        Direct Mail/Promotion Manager

    National Sales Manager
        Regional Sales Managers
            Divisional Sales Managers
            Sales
                Representatives
    Director of Customer Relations
        College Store Relations Manager
        Faculty Relations Manager

Because Marketing bridges Editorial and Sales, let's begin with that group.

Marketing Managers

The role of marketing managers—most of whom previously were sales representatives—varies from publisher to publisher. In some companies, marketing managers handle all marketing functions for one or more disciplines—including market research, advertising, and direct mail. In others, their primary responsibility is limited to preparing the materials used by the sales staff on campus and at sales meetings. In both cases, marketing managers are the key people in developing a comprehensive plan for marketing a discipline or a product.

Let's look at some of a representative marketing manager's broad range of responsibilities:

Marketing Managers' Responsibilities for Selling

- Obtain product information from editorial and from market research.
- Prepare product information fact sheets for sales reps.
- Prepare product information for catalogs.
- Prepare sales kits to be used by sales reps for major titles.
- Assist sales reps to close adoptions on campus.
- Conduct product presentations at national and regional sales meetings.
- Prepare special promotions as needed.
- Staff booths at national and regional discipline conventions.
- Ensure accuracy and effectiveness of direct mail and advertising.

Market Research: Marketing managers begin gathering information and doing market research very early in the publishing process. They may become involved as early as the contract negotiations, especially in a competitive signing situation. They certainly bring their knowledge of markets to bear as an acquisitions editor lays plans for a discipline. The marketing manager may suggest, for example, that a lower-level text or a CD-ROM for a specific market segment be done.

When a project is put under contract, the marketing manager usually receives information about the signing—at the very least, the course for the project, the physical specifications, and the publication date. Especially when a large, introductory project is signed, the marketing manager looks several years down the road and begins preliminary planning. This planning often entails market research into, for example, the kind of ancillary products needed. That market research may be as simple as surveying what the competition has and doing some on-campus interviews or as complex as a full-fledged market research questionnaire costing tens of thousands of dollars.

From this earliest information, the marketing manager begins to plan a strategy for communicating with both the sales staff and the instructors. A critical document is a fact sheet for the sales staff.

Fact Sheets: A fact sheet for a title may be as brief as a half-page outline or many pages long. It contains such basic information as a table of contents, the physical specifications, publication date, price, and package. It also often lists the most important features and benefits, as well as giving information about competition. Often, these fact sheets, which are intended only for the sales reps' eyes, form the basis for catalogs.

Catalogs: Catalogs often contain much of the same information as fact sheets, but because they are intended as a selling tool, the presentation is quite different. Catalogs may be used only by sales reps, in which case they usually replace the fact sheets, or they may be distributed at discipline conventions or mailed to a selected audience—selected because both the unit cost and the postage are quite high. Catalogs for distribution are usually produced for only one discipline, since the person receiving it teaches only that discipline. Marketing managers must determine what titles are to be included, how much copy will be given for each, how frontlist and backlist are presented and labeled, and whether color will be used.

Cost: The unit cost and postage for a catalog could easily be $3–5 for each mailing, and if that catalog were mailed to, say, the 30,000 instructors in psychology or the 33,000 instructors of freshman English composition, a publisher could spend $100,000–150,000 just mailing out a catalog for one discipline. For that reason, as we noted above, the catalogs are usually sent to a limited list.

Sales Kits: Sales kits are specialized material usually prepared only for titles with the greatest sales potential on each list. They tend to be very classy pieces, because they are the main material from which reps presell a title. Sometimes they are self-contained folders, sometimes they are notebooks, sometimes they are a print and video package. In essence, marketing managers try to include everything a rep needs to know to sell the title. The tricky balancing act is to have enough but not so much that it is formidably large or hard to use. All the items found briefly on a fact sheet are given in great detail. There is usually especially detailed information on competitive titles. If the title is a revision, there are lists of past users.

Cost: Sales kits for an important title could cost a publisher $10,000–20,000.

Campus Visits: During the height of the adoption period, marketing managers spend a great deal of time on campus, helping reps to work book fairs and to close large adoptions. When an adoption committee requests that a presentation be made, the marketing manager may be the key presenter. When working on campus during this period, the rep and the marketing manager often work separately so that they can see more people in more departments. Further, the marketing managers' experiences on campus during this critical period give them invaluable information about the marketplace in general and the new title specifically. Often, as a result of being on campus, a marketing manager will send out to sales reps additional information that seems to be needed.

Sales Meetings: In many ways, the first important selling situation takes place at a sales meeting. It is there that a marketing manager must make such a persuasive case for his or her list that the sales staff will want to sell that list rather than another discipline. This motivational factor is a critically important part of sales meetings. The marketing manager and editor of a large project may share in the presentation; often the presentation is multimedia, with lots of bells and whistles; for very competitive courses, the authors of a new title may run a workshop to train the sales reps. For the introduction of a major new title, such as an introductory accounting package, as much as 15–20 percent of the presentation time at even a large publisher's sales meeting may be given over to a single title.

On the surface, it appears that the purpose of the sales meeting is to inform and instruct the sales reps about new product. But what's really going on is the attempt to fill their hearts with confidence and their minds with dollar signs. The point is to really get them fired up.

Special Promotions and Conventions: Marketing managers create special promotions and themes carried throughout a marketing campaign—coffee mugs, tote bags, posters, anything that keeps the name of a title or publisher in front of a decisionmaker. Special promotions often are introduced at discipline conventions or at sales meetings, where reps may be given a T-shirt with the theme. A great favorite was a shirt for reps touting a new book with a special binding. The shirt said: "FLIPS OPEN . . . LIES FLAT."

Even if the promotion is primarily for a convention, reps usually also carry extras with them on campus. One particularly effective, and expensive, special promotion item was a handsomely bound daybook/calendar, with a map and list of restaurants for the convention city in the back. The publisher's name and key title were tastefully present. Conventiongoers especially seem to appreciate humor and food. The two were combined by one publisher, who had a large tray of Chinese fortune cookies. All had the same message: "There's a wonderful new text in your future" with the name of its book.

Marketing managers are also responsible for ensuring the accuracy and effectiveness of advertising and direct mail materials. Even if they are not directly managing these functions, they play a critical role in planning the marketing campaign of which they are part.

Advertising

The value of journal advertising is sometimes debated in a publishing company, with the sales staff feeling that it's of limited value and the editorial staff maintaining that it is very important. In a sense, they are both right if one considers where most space advertising is placed.

Space advertising is generally found in two places: specific discipline journals and convention programs. Editors maintain that a schedule of repeated ads in the most important journals of a discipline introduce titles and reinforce through repetition the image of the cover, the authors' names, and the fact that the title exists or will exist. And not the least important, many editors believe that journal ads are the most effective way to keep a publisher's name and image in front of the faculty for a discipline. These editors repeatedly state that a full advertising program is of invaluable help in signing new authors—that often the hidden factor in a competitive signing situation is how frequently the prospective author has seen ads for the competing companies. Such authors are used to seeing advertising and reviews for trade books and therefore expect to see them for their college title, although, as we have noted before, no professor will adopt a title on the basis of an ad or review without actually seeing the product.

Sales reps often say that journal advertising is fine for introducing new titles and building some cover recognition but that they do not know of any instances of adoptions coming as the direct result of advertising alone. Where they do find advertising especially helpful is in discipline convention programs. Often, professors systematically go through these programs and mark the ads for titles they want to consider for adoption. Such ads get them into the publishers' booths, where marketing and sales staff can pitch the particular title of interest as well as other related titles. The convention requests for examination copies are a very valuable source of names for sales reps to do follow-up sales calls.

Advertising may be created by an inhouse staff working under a promotion manager, or it may be created on the outside by freelance writers and designers or an agency under the direction of a marketing manager.

Costs: Publishers spend on average only a fraction of a percentage of their net sales dollars on space advertising—only about 15 percent, on average, of what they spend on direct mail.

Direct Mail

Direct mail is just what it sounds like: mail sent directly to a potential adopter. This "mail" may be something as simple as a computerized letter, a catalog, or something as complex as a classy full-color brochure with sample pages that costs hundreds of thousands of dollars.

Small companies with few sales reps often rely more heavily on direct mail than do companies with large numbers of reps who can personally reach many professors. A typical brochure usually has the cover on the outside to build recognition so that the prof will remember the cover when an examination copy arrives. After some brief selling copy describing key features, a table of contents is given—and this often lets professors know whether they are even interested in examining a copy of the book or disk. If there was a previous edition, a list of adopters is often given, and there usually is a reply card for requesting an examination copy.

In direct-mail advertising, the effectiveness of the piece is directly related to the specificity of the mailing list. Out in the world at large, a 1 percent response rate is considered outstanding. In college publishing, the response rate—measured as an expression of interest on a response card, usually requesting an examination copy—may be above 15 percent for a really interesting new product, created by a well-known person for a relatively small upper-level market when the mailing list is very accurate for that market. In one example, a brochure for a new contemporary drama anthology was sent to 6,000 professors identified as teaching drama in English departments; and the response rate was excellent—about 16%. In comparison, a mailing to a general list of 30,000 English composition teachers for a revised edition of a handbook got less than a 10% response. Interestingly, a study showed that sales representatives had sent examination copies of both books to about 80% of the professors who eventually adopted them, but the reps generally felt that the brochures had been helpful to their efforts.

The way that mailing lists are created is an example of the circular nature of selling in the college market: The best mailing lists are generated by sales representatives. The names of respondees to a mailing in turn are sent to the sales representatives, who approve the sending of an examination copy and later call on the respondees personally as strong leads for potential adoption.

Direct mail, like advertising, may be handled by an inhouse promotion department or by the marketing manager, working with inhouse and freelance staff.

Costs: Publishers spend an average of 1.4 percent of their total net sales on direct mail. For the industry as a whole, using the most recent statistics, that's more than $12 million.

As we've seen, one of the most important roles of direct mail is to generate a list of professors requesting examination copies.

Examination Copies

All studies have shown that by far the most important factor in an adoption is accurate sampling—that is, the sending of examination copies—to professors by sales reps, which is why publishers invest so heavily in sampling.

Samples can be generated in two ways: First, a professor requests the copy at a convention or in response to an ad or mailing; these requests usually must be approved by the sales representative before the copy is sent. Or, second, the sales representative sends it. In the ideal situation, a sales rep interviews a professor who expresses interest in and requests a copy of one or more titles of interest.

People sometimes complain that publishers do blind sampling, but there's no such thing as *blind* sampling. Reps sometimes do send copies to people they have not interviewed, on the basis of what is sometimes called *informed* sampling. Let's set the situation in which that happens: A rep is on Campus X or in Department Y for only one day that semester—let's say on a Tuesday. She calls on as many people as time and circumstances permit, but it's clear that she can't see everyone on that one day either because there are too many or because half of them have office hours only on Monday, Wednesday, and Friday, the days they're on campus to teach. What the sales rep does is talk to the course coordinators and department chairs about who would be interested in given titles. Also, when she's talking with someone who is interested in a particular title, she always asks who else in the department should see this title. As a last step, she reviews her history of past sampling to see who in this department has in the past requested titles like this one; in fact, this is usually also the first step, because those people are often the first professors a rep tries to see.

Reps do not sample "promiscuously." It would cost them too much. Reps are given maximum quotas for each title and must ensure that those limited numbers of copies go to the most promising prospective adopters or they're liable to end up as a so-called used book and displace a sale, which hits reps where it hurts most: in their wallets.

Costs: The sending of free copies is a huge expense for publishers, the largest single marketing expense except for the total costs for a field sales staff. Publishers spend on average about 3.3 percent of their net sales on the unit cost and postage for examination copies—nearly $30 million. Unfortunately, that cost reflects only the sending of free copies; when professors sell these copies to the so-called used-book wholesalers, who in turn sell them as used books, the estimated cost to publishers is an estimated $200 million in displaced sales, to say nothing of the royalties authors are denied for use of their intellectual property.

Sales

The accurate sending of examination copies is probably the single most important responsibility of a sales representative, but it is part of a much larger process. Sales reps usually report to divisional sales managers, who manage about ten reps. The divisional managers in turn report to regional sales managers—most typically there are three, one each for the East, Midwest, and West sales staffs. Regional managers report to the national sales manager, who has overall responsibility for coordinating all the efforts in the sales area.

The sales management team usually works together to set budgets for both the sales and the expenses of each year, as well as setting policy for such issues as bonuses, territory size, sampling quotas, and training. Essentially, all sales managers—national, regional, or divisional—have responsibility for hiring, training, and supervising the people who report to them. In the case of sales representatives, the training is an onerous task.

Before we look at the selling cycle, let's take just a moment and look at the reps. Who are these people anyway, and how did they get there?

Sales Representatives

Many years ago, most new sales reps were recent college graduates—usually English majors who wanted to be editors—and they were told that they had to be sales reps first. Many of them were from the city where the publisher's headquarters was located, and they went out on the road to get that necessary sales experience.

One of the things that happened was that many of them liked the rep's job so much that they couldn't be dragged into the office in New York or Boston or Chicago. In recent years, reps are often recruited through classified advertising in the sales territory to be filled, and the ads may be listed under Sales or Publishing or both. Very often today, new reps have had some previous selling experience and are looking for a career in sales.

The **average** field sales rep:
• Has a sales territory of roughly $900,000 in annual net sales
• Costs the publisher (compensation, travel expenses, free   copies) about $97,200 (10.8% of sales) a year
• Samples free copies costing about $30,000 annually

A sales rep is responsible for a sales territory, and although the dollar base of about $900,000 is fairly common, the geography of sales territories varies considerably from publisher to publisher. For one small publisher, the Northwest sales territory consisted of Washington, Oregon, Utah, Idaho, Montana, Wyoming, and Nevada; this rep got home about once every six weeks. For one large publisher, the hard-side disciplines at the University of Michigan was a sales territory, and that sales rep got home every night. The average sales base for a territory, then, is about $900,000; and the average cost of putting a rep on the road—including salary and bonus, travel, and free copies—is about 10.8 percent of net sales, or about $97,200. Of the $97,200 that it costs to put the average rep in the field, just about $30,000 is the cost of that rep's free copies.

To best appreciate how a sales staff functions, we shall look at, first, the selling cycle of a year, then look at a day in the life of a sales rep.

Annual Sales Cycle

- August: Sales meeting
- September–December: Sell second-semester titles; presell spring titles; clean lists for sampling
- January: Sales meeting
- January–June: Sell for fall adoptions
- July–August: Follow-up selling; vacation; prepare for sales meeting

August Sales Meeting: For most sales staffs, the selling year begins at the August sales meeting. Some companies use this meeting as an opportunity for focused regional selling training, but most publishers have a national meeting with two primary purposes: to train the sales staff in product knowledge and to pump them up for the coming academic year. Sales meetings often have whole-group meetings, where presentations of the most important new titles are made, as well as smaller regional or divisional group meetings for more intensive training in either content or selling strategies for a single title or for a discipline.

Sometimes the content and the motivational sessions are combined. At one memorable sales meeting where a new English handbook was being introduced, a New York publisher took advantage of the aspiring theater people on staff and produced a thirty-minute musical called "My Fair Handbook," whose broadly played songs and dances covered all the major features of the handbook and its authors. It was recorded on audiotape so that the reps could play it when they were driving to campus. And they did.

With the advent of multimedia, the presentations are often quite exceptional, entertaining, and informational. There also are usually softball or volleyball games, dinners, parties, and excursions. Sound like fun? Well, it is. But think about the other aspects of the meeting: to master a list of perhaps several hundred new titles, to be able to keep them straight from each other, to learn at least their major features, and to have a sense of the competition. Reps do absorb that kind of information for eight or more hours a day at a sales meeting. That's why the presentations of the big books are so entertaining: it's to wake reps up and get their attention.

When reps leave an August meeting, they're expected to have a game plan for their fall campus visits, to know the main features of the major titles and their competition, and to have all the information they need to learn the other titles—and to sell them—from the first day on campus, in about two weeks for most reps.

The amount of information that they are exposed to and expected to know by the end of a sales meeting—so much paper that their luggage will be overweight on the plane—is daunting to the most seasoned reps. It turns the new reps into Bambi in the Headlights. For that reason, there often are special training sessions for all new reps preceding the August meeting, as well as on-campus training with their managers immediately after. For these new reps, their first days on campus seem successful if they can just find the campus and figure out where to park their cars without getting a ticket.

Fall Selling: During the fall, sales representatives have three major responsibilities: First, immediately to sell titles that are primarily used in the next semester or quarter, before the adoption decision date sometime around October 1–15. This means that a rep needs to somehow get to all of his or her major campuses before that date for a first pass. Reps prioritize the new titles for their territories and schedule their campus travel to try to get to as many campuses as possible where there are sales for the next term.

The second major responsibility is to presell important new titles being published for adoption in the spring for the following academic year. This includes identifying potential adopters and ordering examination copies for them. Increasingly, publishers are bringing out these important titles early enough in the fall that reps can actually sell from the book or disk itself. During this time, the critical groundwork is laid for getting the big adoptions during the narrow window in the spring.

The third—tedious and time-consuming—task in the fall is to update faculty lists. Companies have various policies about how frequently these lists get "cleaned" and some publishers have inhouse staff who do it. In any case, especially for a publisher's major disciplines, someone has to contact departmental secretaries and verify that the names on the list are correct, for these lists determine who the rep calls on and who receives direct-mail pieces.

One advantage in having reps personally check their lists with departmental secretaries is that it's a great opportunity to pick up useful information—everything from who's on an adoption committee to the pronunciation of the new chair's name.

January Sales Meeting: Most publishers have a national sales meeting beginning the first week in January, usually in a warm, inviting place, for this is the relative calm before the storm.

The general goals are the same as for the August meeting, though whereas the August meeting may emphasize product information, the January meeting tends to emphasize selling strategies. All the information that was gleaned during the fall is consolidated. Here is the opportunity to get from editors answers to questions that came up in the fall. Here is the time to compare information about new competitors for the major titles.

Reps must leave this meeting feeling they've got all the sales tools they need to go out and win every sale. They really have to be pumped up, because the next four months are going to be hell.

January–June: How casual it sounds to say, "Sell for fall adoptions," like it's some kind of leisure activity, perhaps croquet.

The actual image that comes to mind are honey gatherers, swathed in heavy cloth "armor" trying to get honey out of a comb, while a swarm of bees circle, stinging and trying to fight you off.

At this point, let's consider a day in the life of a rep during this period.

A Day in the Life of a Sales Representative

March 6:

4:30–9:00: Drive to next campus; dinner enroute

9:00–11:20: Input list corrections and sampling from day's work

11:20–1:00: Lay out calling for tomorrow

March 7:

6:30: Wake-up call

7:15: Arrive on campus; parking

8:00–8:45: College store; review lists

8:45: Administration Building for schedules

9:00–4:45: 26 interviews in biology, accounting, political science, English

4:45–6:00: College store; check stacks

6:15–7:00: Dinner

7:00–10:00: Inputting sampling; planning next day

The first thing you notice is that a day in the life extends over two days. It begins the evening of March 6. Tomorrow the rep will be on campus for the first time this semester at one of his smaller state colleges that is some distance from the heart of his territory, and he'll be here for two days. Most of the freshman-level decisions are made by committees, including English, where one committee chooses a handbook, but all the readers used are individual choice, and there is huge potential there.

Tonight the rep arrived at his motel at about 9 pm after driving from his previous campus. He has eaten on the road, so he can turn to his paperwork as soon as he has called his wife and gotten settled in his room. He first has to finish the paperwork from today's school. Now that his sales staff is using laptop computers, he can input the sampling himself, which speeds up the delivery of exam copies but takes him more time in the evenings.

Although he was up to date yesterday, it still takes him more than two hours to input the sampling and faculty corrections that turned up today. Using the modem in his room, he transmits the sampling. After several busy signals, he gets through and also picks up his e-mail. There are six messages. The two from his manager mean more work: One is a request for a report on the use of videodisks in the social sciences in his territory. The other is a request to arrange for the English editor to call with him to help sell his new American literature anthology at his biggest school. The other four messages are about open adoptions on other campuses that he'll have to follow up by telephone tomorrow. At about 11:20 pm he turns to tomorrow's school.

The rep laid good groundwork on his last visit to campus, in the fall. He knows that there are open unit adoptions in accounting, biology, American government, and psychology; that all the reader adoptions in English are up for grabs and he has strong candidates; and that he has that strong new American literature title. He decides to start in biology, since that faculty tends to be in early on this campus, then go to accounting for most of the day, then political science. This season he's spending almost 30 percent of his time in accounting departments, so the second day, he'll go back to accounting to see any committee members he's missed, then go to psychology. He'll go in and out of English as he criss-crosses the campus, catching as many of those individual-choice profs as possible. At the end of the day, he'll hit the other departments and try to find out where things stand and catch people as he can. He puts all his faculty lists and sales materials in order and goes to sleep about 1 am.

When the wake-up call comes at 6:30, the rep is jolted. He lies there confused for a minute, listening for his kids, then he remembers where he is, what the call is. He has given up alarm clocks; by March he was turning them off in his sleep. He showers and dresses conservatively—he's spending most of his time in the Accounting Department, so the tie stays on today. He reaches campus by 7:15 and goes to the security office for a parking permit, and he's early enough to get one of the spaces that is relatively close to the college store and the center of the campus. He picks up the student newspaper and reads it while he eats breakfast in the nearly deserted cafeteria.

When the college store opens at 8, he is there. The text manager, with whom he has become friendly, says that he knows of no problems with that publisher and gives the rep a printout of orders. Before the rep looks through the listings, he chats for a few minutes with the text manager about what is happening in some of the departments. In that conversation he learns that the political science department has decided to stay with their current American government text and has already placed the order for the fall. But they intensely dislike the international relations text they just adopted and will be changing for the fall, despite their usual practice of keeping a title for two years. The rep notes the names of the international relations faculty he wants to see. It also seems that the pressure is on to make adoption decisions earlier than usual, and reps from a number of companies have been around earlier in the week talking to accounting committee members. The rep finds that several of his titles have been picked up for this semester, and he makes a note to stop by and thank the profs for the business. He also notices that there were adoptions of some competitors' texts he does not know, so he decides to come back at the end of the day and look through the shelves to familiarize himself with them.

By 9 am the rep is in the biology department office, confirming with the departmental secretary who is on the adoption committee, checking office hours, and in general just schmoozing and seeking gossip about who has influence in the decision, whether the department really has gotten funding for a computer lab and simulation software. Thus begins a kaleidoscope of a day of knocking on doors, presenting books, occasionally running out to his car for examination copies if a decision is imminent; returning phone calls from yesterday;

generally playing the role of benign and generous sleuth on the trail of the accounting committee.

For lunch he grabs a tuna sandwich from a machine in the basement of the biology department on his second run there. In the fall he always had time to eat in the student union, a real treat because of the food sciences program here, but at this time of year he is lucky to get a sandwich, even if it, like everything else in this building, smells of formaldehyde. In midmorning he had stopped in the Administration Building for a class schedule, which he looks over as he eats. He is struck by the increased number of sections of social-problems courses and decides to try to stop by the sociology department to see what is happening and especially to follow up on the report his manager wants about the use of video.

By 4:45 he has conducted twenty-six interviews and there is not another faculty member to be found, so he heads back to the college store to look over the books in the stacks. By 6:30 pm he is in the local Friendly's Restaurant, eating clam chowder and reviewing his day. He is actually pretty excited about how many people he found today and feels his chances are really good for two of the unit adoptions. But he is feeling lonely, and tired, and he still has several hours of inputting sampling.

Tomorrow he'll get up and do it again. The only difference is that it will be Friday, and he'll be driving home, three hours away, when he finishes calling. He'll work four or five hours on Saturday, doing Friday's sampling and sending off some follow-up letters to potential adopters, but he'll have a lot of Sunday free before he gets in the car Sunday evening for the drive to the western part of the state, where he'll be on campus bright and early Monday.

July–August: The annual spring madness usually begins with the big unit adoptions, then winds down with upper-level and individual-choice decisions sometime after mid-April, depending upon the territory. Sales reps tend to be numb with exhaustion by that point but usually have to wrap up their year-end reports and work. Again, depending upon the territory, they fit in a vacation along with some summer selling.

In some territories, decisions about course staffing aren't made until summertime, and there's often the opportunity to catch new faculty and get some adoptions. Summer is also a fine time for selling ancillaries, and many reps do an exceptional job revisiting their major adoptions to sell study guides and other ancillaries. Most reps also have some kind of special summer project—perhaps researching the offerings for a specific course or discipline throughout the sales territory.

All too soon, the paper starts arriving for the August sales meeting, and the reps themselves become students as they prepare for the coming selling cycle, beginning with the sales meeting. They've come full circle.

Why would someone seek, and stay in, a job that is so grueling, so stressful, so lonely? It does take a special kind of person, and publishers have very keen ways of evaluating candidates for sales openings to try to find those people. Reps who stay in this job usually say that they love the independence and autonomy that they have in determining how and where they spend their time; they love the hunt, the chase, the competition; they love working in a way that their payoff—their bonuses—are directly related to how hard and how smart they work. And finally, many of them talk about how special it is to be a sales *representative*—they literally represent their company on campus and perform a service as well as a sales function that involves a product that they are proud of.

Customer Relations

Publishers have a variety of structures for dealing with all their customers' needs, and they have different titles for who does what. Thus, these are general descriptions of three broad areas of customer relations in a publishing company. One interacts with faculty and two with stores.

Faculty Relations: The staff who interact by telephone with faculty usually report within the sales department, and their primary responsibility is to see that examination copies for potential adopters, desk copies for adopters, and ancillaries get to professors. They may receive calls directly from professors or may get calls from sales representatives who need to expedite some material. Most often these staff are in the home office, but sometimes they work out of regional offices or work in conjunction with telemarketers.

Customer Service: The people most often called the customer service department usually work in the corporate operations area, in the order entry or fulfillment department. Their primary responsibility is to take orders from college stores and bookstores and to deal with any problems that arise in fulfillment. Even when they report within a corporate area, there is a system that alerts the college sales area of any problems involving shipments.

College Store Relations: Beginning about ten years ago, college publishers started taking significant steps to improve relationships with college stores. The sales rep is the person who most often interacts with stores, but if a rep is on campus only once during a term and misses the text manager, communication isn't what it should be. Some of the steps that have been taken in this effort to improve relations include:

- *On-campus training of new reps.* Managers spend their first days on campus with new reps modeling "repdom." The first stop is the college store, where reps learn both what tasks they should accomplish and what appropriate conduct is.
- *Training sessions for reps at sales meetings.* Many publishers invite store personnel to

attend sessions at their national sales meetings and participate in the training.

- *College store advisory groups.* Many publishers have established advisory panels of store personnel, representing two- and four-year schools in all regions of the country. This panel may participate in training sessions at national sales meetings, and they also serve as a sounding board for policy matters the publisher has in place or is considering. The advisory group may meet with the publisher at the annual meeting of the National Association of College Stores (NACS) and perhaps at other times of year. In an effort for better understanding, advisory-group members sometimes go on sales calls with local reps.

- *Publisher participation in rush.* A number of sales reps, again to better understand the store's challenges, participate regularly by working "rush," although doing so is very problematic for some, especially smaller, publishers. For the first time, several years ago, a number of managers, including presidents of college publishing companies, also worked rush.

- *Newsletters or other special communications.* These communications usually give current information about new editions, prices, and ordering policies. They also tend to give personal information about the people at the other end of the phone.

- *Participation at regional and national NACS meetings.* Many years ago, only a few publishers attended regional NACS meetings, but today many publishers attend ten or more a year. At regional and national meetings, publishers participate in educational sessions and fundraising efforts such as silent auctions.

- *Special services.* Publishers have put in place a number of seasonal, permanent, and experimental programs to better relations with stores. Some of these have included hotlines, special rush shipment arrangements, putting in place the Pubnet ordering system, extended hours, joint marketing options, and value-added campaigns.

- *Appointment of a store-relations manager.* Many publishers have appointed a seasoned store-relations manager. The earliest people to hold this position had backgrounds working in college stores and bookstores; some of the more recent managers have had experience as college sales reps. These managers usually plan that publisher's participation with stores, draft policy guidelines, and establish and frequently administer special programs.

- *Joint NACS–AAP sessions.* In addition to special sessions at NACS meetings, the head of one college house participates as a member of the NACS board, and members of the AAP Higher Education Executive Council meet at regular intervals with members of the NACS board.

Throughout the acquisition and development processes, editors work to best serve the needs of two of their customers: students and professors. Through steps such as those outlined above, publishers strive to meet the needs of the only customer who regularly purchases directly from them.

5 THE FINANCES OF COLLEGE PUBLISHING

We use symbols all the time. Without really thinking about it, we slow down the car when we catch sight of a red, octagonal road sign. The word on that sign, *STOP*, is the most common kind of symbol that we use everyday: words. Numbers, too, are symbols that are inseparable from our daily experience. Interestingly, written numbers are actually historically older than written words. Writing emerged more than 5,000 years ago among the Sumerians, who developed pictographs to keep accounting records. Archeological finds show that they had already developed a system for writing down numbers.

Although numbers basically are fairly impersonal symbols, they too can have great emotional impact within their context, or with the addition of another simple symbol: the dollar sign.

A great many people in publishing started out as English majors, and they went toward publishing because they loved to read. Some even wanted to write The Great American novel. So what happened when they got into publishing? They were given a sales territory—and many of them went through severe culture shock at the very *idea* of selling. But many of them discovered that they love the sales rep's job so much that it's now hard to get them into the home office to do the editorial work that most of them were initially aiming for. While they are sales reps, they get good practice working with numbers: expense reports, sampling budgets, sales, even returns. But the work in the field really cannot prepare them for the kinds of numbers they work with as editors.

To look at the finances of publishing, we're going to go through the kind of model that a new editor might be introduced to, then we'll look more closely at some of the details.

Every year, the Association of American Publishers (AAP) gathers certain kinds of statistical information from its member publishers and makes the compilation available. The way the AAP presents these statistics is the way most publishers look at their overall operation. It's also the way most editors look at the disciplines they're responsible for and even at some individual titles in a discipline. Publishers may internally account for some of the expenses differently— such as how they handle the one-time prepress expenses called plant costs—but they all *report* the numbers in the same way to the AAP so that they can compare their performance against the industry as a whole and against other publishers of about the same size.

Let's first look at the broad categories reported:

AAP Operating Data for College Publishers

> Net Sales
> – "Cost of Sales"
> =Gross Margin
>
> + Other Income
> – Publishing and Operating Expenses
> =Income from Operations

Net sales minus a group of expenses called **cost of sales** equals **gross margin**—a very important measurement, or hurdle rate, for profitability. **Gross margin** plus **other income** less **publishing and operating expenses** yields the **income from operations**.

Note that these operating expenses do not include all corporate charges, such as legal and accounting fees.

Let's first look more closely at gross margin, with the actual numbers for 1993, the most recent available. In addition to dollars, publishers also look very hard at each item as a percentage of net sales, which gives them a constant way of looking at and comparing one year against another or one discipline against another or even one large package against another.

Gross Margin for AAP Publishers—1993

	$(000s)	% of Net Sales
Gross Sales	$1,105,092	128.3
−Returns	243,972	28.3
= Net Sales	861,120	100.0
Cost of Sales		
Paper, printing,		
binding,		
duplicating	165,434	19.4
Royalties	121,644	14.2
Unspecified	2,501	
−Total Cost of Sales	289,579	33.6
=Gross Margin	571,541	66.4

Let's look more closely at each of these line items:

Gross sales are the total number of units shipped out as the result of orders from stores. This is the number of units that a publisher must manufacture and have in the warehouse after all examination and desk copies—that is, free copies—have been accounted for. As you can see, the gross sales are 128.3% of net sales. What's the difference? You got it: Returns.

Returns are just what they're called. To re-word an old cliché: Gone today, here tomorrow. As you can see, returns in 1993 amounted to 28.3 percent of net sales, or about $244 million. These are units that were manufactured and sent out and have been returned to the warehouse. A couple of points: first, they had to be manufactured; second, they may or may not be usable for reshipment. Returns percentages have been creeping up steadily for years, for various reasons, including student resistance to buying, increased used-books sales, and more flexible returns policies of publishers.

When we subtract returns from gross sales we get net sales.

Net sales, simply, are the sales publishers get paid for—it works out to about 78 percent of what they ship. Because net sales are the ones publishers get paid for, this is the number that is looked at as the basis for profitability calculations.

One thing that does not show up in these numbers is the cost of money over time. Sometimes books that are printed in December are shipped as examination copies in January; they're adopted in April; the students' copies are shipped in August; they are paid for by the store in November, except for those being kept at the store in a held-books program, which may be paid for in March. So the bulk of the books may be paid for nearly a year, sometimes even more, after the publisher paid to print them. With this in mind, publishers try to print in the most economical quantities, but the more units are printed, the cheaper is each unit—especially for large or color books, factors in the next category, paper, printing, and binding, or PP&B.

PP&B is by far the largest direct expense on print products. And with the enormous increases in paper prices recently, it is really skyrocketing—the numbers for 1995 will show a huge jump here. There simply isn't enough price flexibility to absorb these increases.

The "cruelest" aspect of PP&B is that publishers pay for it on every copy they print or manufacture, whether the unit is sold, given away, or sitting in the warehouse. The numbers here reflect only the units that are sold. Mostly, they're books, but electronic products that are sold are included, though they usually have a lower relative unit cost.

Royalties are percentages of net receipts paid to authors, as well as sometimes to series editors or special kinds of consultants. Thirty years ago, royalties were based on list prices, but most college publishers then converted to contracts based on net receipts for a number of reasons: paying royalties on a list price affected their ability especially to negotiate special prices for, say, international sales. In recent years, moreover, many publishers have gone to net pricing and do not set the selling prices.

Royalties vary greatly depending upon the kind of product involved. For print product, few publishers go above 15 percent of net receipts, but there are exceptions in both directions. If, for example, a publisher is putting out an anthology with high permissions costs and limited sales and is itself paying all of the permissions costs, the royalty may be quite low. The royalties for salable ancillaries are also low because the margins on them are quite tight. For an art history book, where the cost of both image rights and manufacturing are extraordinarily high, the royalty may be much lower.

In the cases where a book has enormous potential, the royalty rate may have jumps based on sales. The royalty rate may start at 12.5% or even 15%, then jump up several percentage points at the breakeven point for the publisher, and in some cases may have a third jump for significant sales.

Usually, there is an advance given against royalties for signing, especially in competitive situations. In many cases the advance is a few thousand dollars; in a few notable cases, it is in seven figures. Once again, the cost of money over time is not in these figures, but interest expense for money out in advances can be considerable. Theoretically, advances earn out when a project begins to sell.

It's virtually impossible to make any kind of royalty generalization for electronic product because there are so many different arrangements, including doing considerable work in house. Usually, whatever royalty is paid on electronic product, the publisher will take into consideration the manufacturing costs and aim for at least the same gross margin as for print products.

Unspecified is a small category, a kind of catchall for publishers. For some, it includes some inventory writedown costs, especially those involving free ancillaries after the first year.

Gross Margin

Overall, then, gross margin is a very important measurement of profitability for publishers. It is important to note that not all publishers internally calculate gross margin as is done in the AAP statistics: Some publishers also include plant cost, which we'll turn to below. But no matter where plant is calculated, publishers are looking for particular kinds of gross margin numbers.

As a generalization, successful small publishers tend to have higher gross margins that do large publishers because small publishers often publish kinds of books that have lower PP&B costs and lower royalties.

How do larger publishers manage to achieve solid gross margins? In many ways it's like setting up a balanced stock portfolio, with blue chips and some riskier investments. Another way to think of it is an analogy to nature: If you have an environmental niche with only one kind of plant in it and the right kind of locust comes along, it's wiped out. The most stable environment is one that is mixed and balanced. Most large publishers take the same kind of approach in the balance of disciplines for which they publish, and also in the mixture of products in any discipline. Further, publishers have different structures and economies of scale for operating expenses, which we'll consider closely. To see how gross margins are related to size, let's compare smaller companies with $20–50 million sales to those having more than $100 million in sales.

Gross Margin and Size of AAP Publishers—1993

	All AAP	$20–50 million	Over $100 million
Net Sales	100.0%	100.0%	100.0%
–PP&B	19.4	16.9%	19.6%
–Royalty	14.2	10.4	15.0
=GM	66.4%	72.7%	65.4%

As you can see, the smaller publishers pay considerably less in PP&B and in royalty than do larger publishers. We can see how this is achieved by looking at the gross margins of two successful, fictional but representative titles that might be published by the companies in these categories. One is an introductory biology text, the other a freshman composition reader.

Gross Margin and Type of Product

	AAP	Reader	Biology
Net Sales	100.0%	100.0%	100.0%
PP&B	19.4%	14.3%	19.8%
Royalty	14.2%	12.5%	14.0%
Gross Margin	66.4%	73.2%	66.2%

In fact, publishers in both size groups probably have individual titles that include gross margins like the biology text's and the reader's. It is simply more likely that a smaller company will have, overall, a smaller proportion of the large introductory product.

Yet interestingly, they are both aiming for the same bottom line. Let's look first at categories of expenses, then see how these expenses affect the bottom line for different sizes of publishers.

Publishing and Operating Expenses

Publishing and Operating Expenses for AAP Publishers—1993

	Thousands of $	% of Net Sales
Plant Costs	$61,301	7.2%
Editorial	53,529	6.3
Production	30,355	3.6
Marketing	163,483	19.1
Fulfillment	37,076	4.3
Gen. & Admin	92,536	10.8
Unspecified	3,310	
Total	$441,590	51.3%

The broad general categories outlined for publishing and operating expenses are by no means the complete costs for all publishers. They do not include, for example, such corporate charges as corporate staff compensation, legal and accounting fees, interest costs, and other charges that are not directly applicable to a particular business segment. They do include the costs that are generally comparable among the AAP's member publishers. Let's look at each.

Plant Costs
Plant costs are the one-time prepress costs incurred from the time a project comes in

until it is actually manufactured. Let's look at the general categories under plant cost—though, once again, there may be some variation in how things are accounted by different publishers.

Major Categories of Plant Costs

Reviewing
Grants
Free-Ancillary Preparation
Permissions (Text and Photo)
Illustration Rendering
Design
Composition (Typesetting)
Proofreading
Indexing
Color Separations
Prepress

Let me very briefly touch on each of these expenses. The costs quoted are very generalized because there is such variation in how something may be handled.

Reviewing is done at several stages, beginning with the first proposal for a project. During development, there are specialist and developmental reviews. And before a project is manufactured, there may be marketing reviews. The cost of reviewing may be as little as $1,000 for the table of contents of an anthology to as much as $300,000 for a major project.

Grants are given to authors, usually for research, manuscript preparation, or assistance in preparing nonsalable ancillaries. Grants may range from zero to tens of thousands of dollars for complex projects.

Permissions costs for books can be very small or monstrous. Text permissions, for example, could run as high as $300,000 for a literature anthology that has a good balance of contemporary works—and that's for use in one edition in North America only. Photo permissions also depend upon what rights are wanted—world rights are about double North American rights—on the size that is to be reproduced, and on whether the photo is black and white or color. Photo permissions for a heavily illustrated book in the social sciences could run several hundred thousand dollars. In terms of permissions costs for electronic rights, they could run from expensive to impossible to obtain under any circumstances. Many of the suppliers of video images are used to their being picked up for commercial uses, and it's sometimes difficult or impossible to get rights for existing material— especially fine art—for electronic reproduction.

Illustration rendering, the line drawings done for a project, could be as inexpensive as $100 for a simple drawing to $1,000 for a complex anatomical drawing.

Design is usually done by freelances. A text design could run from $1,000; a text and cover design for a complex book could be $15,000. Designers also are involved in dummying, or laying out, very complex works. The total design costs on a project, including laying it out, could be as low as $3,000 or as much as $160,0000.

Composition, or typesetting, is an area that is being greatly affected by new technologies. In traditional typesetting, the cost could be as low as $20 or as high as $80 per page. So a complex, thousand-page book in the social science could cost $80,000 for composition. Increasingly, publishers are handling manuscripts in digital form, which significantly reduces the cost of composition.

Proofreading and sometimes copy editing are included in plant cost by some publishers. Proofreading is done for at least two stages. Proofreading costs average $20 per hour, about 5–6 book pages per hour. Thus, that same thousand-page book would cost about $3,400–5,000 at each stage for proofreading. Copy editing would probably run about $8,000–12,000; sometimes this expense is included under Editorial or Production costs, but often it's in plant cost.

Indexing is done after the second stage of proof and usually costs a dollar an entry, for an average of $3,000–8,000. There are excellent computerized programs for creating indexes, but they require additional coding and cannot effectively be used for cross-referencing and conceptual entries where the exact word doesn't appear in the text, so old-fashioned indexers are still the norm.

Color separations must be made of all color photographs to be printed. Although electronic technology and color scanning have advanced considerably, this process remains expensive.

Prepress covers a number of steps, including color separations. The term usually is used to cover the preparation of and stripping up of film from which printing plates are made. The shooting and stripping of text and illustrations for a four-color introductory text could run about $200,000.

Editorial

Editorial costs are primarily the people costs of the editorial department. These costs include salary and benefits, travel, and the cost of reviewing projects that are not put under contract.

Production

Production costs, similarly, are people costs— salary and benefits, and travel. Copy editing costs are often logged in this category if they are not treated as plant cost.

Marketing

Marketing and sales costs are quite complex, and they are the largest single overhead category of expense. The following items are included under the Marketing head:

Marketing Costs

- Sales staff salaries, bonuses, and benefits
- Sales travel (including cars and expenses on the road)
- Marketing/Promotion staff salaries, bonuses, and benefits
- Marketing/Promotion T&E expenses
- Space advertising
- Direct mail
- Free copies and postage
- Free ancillaries, software, films
- Exhibits and conventions

As you can see, publishers spend about $163 million to perform that all-important challenge of getting the right book into the right hands. As part of this effort, publishers spend about 3.3 percent of net sales, or more than $28 million dollars, on the unit cost and postage of free copies.

Fulfillment

Fulfillment costs usually include the corporate order entry, customer service, warehousing, and fulfillment operations. Most publishers have one or more of their own warehouses but smaller companies may not own theirs.

General and Administration

G & A expenses include rent, telephones, electricity, water, heat and air conditioning, postage, and sometimes the compensation of executive officers. As we noted above, the Income from Operations is not an accurate reflection of pre-tax margins because there is great variation in what corporate charges are included or not in the G&A expense.

Income from Operations

Let's look for a moment at these numbers, then consider how these expenses are related to size, and finally look at the bottom line, the effect of all these expenses.

Operating Data for AAP Publishers—1993

	Thousands of $	% of Net Sales
Net Sales	$861,120	100.0%
–Cost of Sales	289,579	33.6
=Gross Margin	$571,541	66.4%
–Pub/Operating Expenses		
Plant Costs	61,301	7.2
Editorial	53,529	6.3
Production	30,355	3.6
Marketing	163,483	19.1
Fulfillment	37,076	4.3
Gen. & Admin	92,536	10.8
Unspecified	3,310	
–Total Pub/Op.	$441,590	51.3%
=Income from Op.	$129,951	15.1%

As you can see, on net sales of $861 million, the pretax income from operations, before corporate charges, is under $130 million—about 15.1%, relatively modest returns for an incredibly complex and challenging business.

Let's look at the numbers one more time to see the effect of size on the almost-bottom line:

Overhead Expenses and Size of AAP Publishers—1993—as a Percentage of Net Sales

	All AAP	$20–50 million	Over $100 million
Plant Costs	7.2%	7.7%	6.3%
Editorial	6.3%	7.6%	5.3
Production	3.6%	3.1%	3.3
Marketing	19.1%	21.5%	19.1
Fulfillment	4.3%	5.5%	4.3
Gen. & Admin	10.8%	10.2%	11.7
Total Pub/Op.	51.3%	55.6%	50.1%

Looking at these publishing and operations expenses, we can easily see the effect of size, some 5.5 percent of net sales difference. This very great difference in expenses is probably the result of two things: First, as we've noted, larger companies tend to publish a higher proportion of large, introductory packages with large sales against which plant cost, for example, is written; related to this, the larger companies tend to rely heavily on personal selling of these large packages, whereas smaller companies spend a higher proportion of their marketing dollar on advertising and direct mail. The second major factor in this 5.5

percent difference is, quite simply, economies of scale. These economies show up in many places—in marketing, in warehousing, in ratio of editors to number of titles.

Let's look now at what is the end point: the bottom line—or the almost-bottom line, as the case may be here.

Income from Operations and Size of AAP Publishers—1993 as a Percentage of Net Sales

	All AAP	$20–50 million	Over $100 million
Net Sales	100.0%	100.0%	100.0%
Gross Margin	66.4%	72.7%	65.4%
–Overhead Exp.	51.3%	55.6%	50.1%
=Income	15.1%	17.1%	15.3%

The point in looking at these numbers is not really to show that being larger or smaller is better or worse. It's that being larger or smaller can affect—not *that*—but *how* publishers make a profit. Looking at these affects of size, then, is an excellent way to begin to use these numbers that make up the very complex finances of publishing. As you can see, for smaller companies the gross margin—which is affected by royalty and paper, printing, and binding—is very strong because of the kinds of products most smaller companies publish. For larger companies, the gross margin takes a real hit from all the big introductory packages, but there are balancing economies of scale in overhead expenses, especially marketing/sales and fulfillment.

The numbers we've looked at here are a picture at one moment in time of the finances of publishing. If we had looked ten or twenty years ago, we would have seen a very different picture. For one thing, as a percentage of net sales, returns and income would have shown a major shift: returns were about 10 percent of net sales lower, and income was about 10 percent higher.

If we could look twenty years into the future, we'd see, I'm sure, an even more dramatic change.

6 THE FUTURE

When we look back at the world of college publishing ten or twenty or thirty years ago, we get a quite different picture than we do today. The first full-color textbook, *Psychology Today*, was published in 1968. It had no free ancillaries—the first test files were still several years away—and with a price of $12, it was $2 over the average market price then. The baby boomers were on campus, and college publishers' sales and profits were skyrocketing. They could sell almost everything they could publish, and sales on an individual title held fairly constant for nearly five years—closer to ten years in some disciplines. Sales reps were called book*men*, and until the early 1970s all of them *were* men, as were the editors, marketing managers, and virtually everyone in management.

If we could look thirty or twenty or even ten years into the future, I'm sure we'd see an even more dramatic difference. We're facing a marketplace with different kinds of students in different places using different kinds of materials. Looking at the stages and functions discussed in earlier chapters, we can begin to see hints of what's emerging.

Editorial Department

The Editorial Department will continue to research markets, to acquire products by putting author teams under contract, and to develop or have developed those products. Although the responsibilities of this department as such will probably change less than others, new technologies will greatly affect the who, how, where, and when of editorial work. In a continuation of a trend already begun, editorial staff will work increasingly in teams with new kinds of members, including graphic, technical, and curriculum specialists, all of whom will function in a role that is nearly authorial.

There undoubtedly will continue to be a "home office," but it is likely that all the members of the editorial team will not be in it. Enhanced communication technology will enable them to interact comfortably from their offices, homes, and campuses, wherever they may be.

No matter what the platforms—most likely print and electronic will be used in different proportions in different situations—the editorial staff will continue to orchestrate the creation of product, for it is the pedagogical enhancement of educational materials that is the irreplaceable role of publishers.

Production/Manufacturing Departments

The Production and Manufacturing Departments will probably be the most dramatically changed in the coming decades as the delivery media for educational materials continue to become increasingly electronic. Many of the changes that we can foresee, in fact, are already well under way. Even when the product is print, its creation will be done so completely digitally that its development will also be its production.

"Manufacturing" not only will encompass some printing and binding and some manufacturing of disks but also will include ensuring the accessibility and security of huge amounts of pedagogically enhanced material available online and via satellite to the large numbers of students who will no longer be found on traditional college campuses as well as to those on campus.

Marketing/Sales Departments

As we've noted, the primary goal of Marketing and Sales is to put the right title into the hands of the right professors at the right time. What we'll increasingly see is that those hands are on keyboards and mouses— elegant and sophisticated digital shopping malls where professors can look closely at the materials they are interested in, probably online, and use menu-driven metering systems to order or download what they want. This process is already under way in the ancillaries that can be accessed via Internet and commercial online services. At conventions, in college stores, and possibly in departments themselves, innovative kiosks and video displays will compete for potential adopters' attention. Reps will be able to show adopters virtually any part of any title on the miniature digital "briefcase" they'll carry and can create instant samples when needed.

Business/Administration/Operations Department

The business planning and budgeting responsibilities will continue, but many operations areas involving order entry and fulfillment will be entirely online. Some aspects of pricing and approaches to profitability will be altered when publishers no longer have to make massive investments in the paper, printing, and binding costs for their entire front list at the time of that adoption window. Because the manufacturing, sampling, and fulfillment costs will be reduced significantly and returns will be minimal, a new pricing model for the pedagogically enhanced information will be created. A first step in this direction was taken in the AAP Higher Education Division's 1995 Strategic Plan, which includes the goal of developing potential models for the industry as a whole, focusing on customer needs regarding product formats, product combinations/transaction sets, and distribution channel approaches.

What will the future hold for educational publishing? Right now trying to determine what it will be is like looking at the reverse side of a tapestry: There are thousands of threads, and many of them do not seem to be tied to anything. When we, as an industry, can reach agreement with our customers about issues such as intellectual property rights, we'll be able to turn the tapestry over and see the pattern.

Today's college publishers will be the focal point of that pattern, for they above all others are best able to provide the pedagogically enhanced content that can be carried by formats barely dreamed of now.

At the 1995 NACS Annual Meeting, James Lichtenberg, Vice-President, Higher Education, AAP, asked attendees three questions that are critical for all of us who in any way work inside of or with college publishing:

"Do you really understand course materials?

"Do you really support them as 'learning' partners for students?

"Do you really promote them?

"If so, you will know how to change as the future arrives . . ."

GLOSSARY

ACQUISITIONS EDITORS Editors responsible for researching markets, signing new products, determining revision cycles for existing titles, and ensuring the profitability of one or more disciplines.

ADHESIVE BINDING A binding in which the pages are held together by glue.

ADVANCES Money given to authors against future royalties, usually limited to some portion of sales expected in the first year.

ANCILLARIES Print or nonprint products intended to enhance a related core product. Some, such as study guides and lab manuals, are usually sold. Others, such as instructors' manuals and computerized tests, are usually given to adopters and potential adopters.

ASSOCIATION OF AMERICAN PUBLISHERS (AAP) The publishing industry's trade association, whose Higher Education Division is concerned with the issues that affect publishers for that market.

BLIND SAMPLING Sending of unrequested examination copies to professors. *See also* INFORMED SAMPLING.

BOUND-BOOK DATE The date that a book comes off the binding line. It may precede the official PUBLICATION DATE and the COPYRIGHT YEAR and may be the date after which examination copies are available though the title is not yet for sale.

COLLATE Put into sequence.

COLOR SEPARATION Scanning color images, such as color photographs, to produce four pieces of film that, using the so-called process-color inks—cyan (blue), magenta (red), yellow, and black—create the full spectrum of colors on a printed page.

COMPOSITE FILM Film for the text, photos, and art integrated electronically or stripped together mechanically in preparation for printing.

COMPOSITION Setting type.

COPY EDITORS Editors responsible for imposing consistent spelling and grammatical usage, coding design elements such as heads and set-off material for the designer, and sometimes checking facts or smoothing language.

COPYRIGHT YEAR The year of the official publication date. Increasingly, college publishers bring out products four or five months earlier than the copyright year in order to presell them.

COST OF SALES A category used by publishers that usually includes costs for paper, printing, binding, duplication, and royalties.

CUSTOMIZED PRODUCT Print or nonprint materials created to a customer's content specifications.

DESK COPY A free copy of print or nonprint material for the use of a professor who has adopted that item for classroom use.

DESKTOP PUBLISHING At a publishing company, having specially trained editors and designers handle the composition and makeup processes inhouse.

DEVELOPMENT EDITORS Editors who direct or execute the development of large-revenue packages in specific discipline areas.

DIRECT MAIL Marketing by sending brochures, flyers, letters, or catalog through the mails to potential customers.

ELECTRONIC PRODUCT Essentially all material that is nonprint, including software, CD-ROMs, videodisks, online services.

EXAMINATION COPY A free copy of print or nonprint material sent to a potential adopter by a sales representative or in response to a request from that potential adopter. Compare DESK COPY.

FOLIO Page number.

GALLEY The first, unpaginated proofs after type has been set; named after the metal trays on which lines of type were set when hot-metal technology was used.

GRANTS Money given outright to authors, usually for purchasing hardware or hiring graduate assistants for research or for preparing nonsalable ancillaries.

GROSS SALES The total number of units ordered by stores, before returns.

HALFTONES Photographs (continuous tones) on which a fine screen has been imposed so that the image can be printed.

INFORMED SAMPLING The sending of unrequested examination copies on the basis of recommendations gathered during sales calls with the recipients' colleagues.

LAUNCH (TRANSMITTAL) MEETING The meeting at which a final manuscript is transmitted for production, during which specifications, budget, schedule, and market issues are confirmed.

NATIONAL ASSOCIATION OF COLLEGE STORES (NACS) The college stores' trade association.

NET SALES Gross sales less returns; what publishers get paid for.

PLANT COST The one-time costs incurred before manufacturing, usually include: reviewing, grants, free-ancillary preparation, text and illustration permissions, illustration rendering, design, composition (typesetting), proofreading, indexing, and PREPRESS.

PP&B Paper, printing, and binding—the unit cost of a print product.

PREPRESS All the production stages that physically convert text and images into a form that can be used to manufacture the product.

PRINTING ON DEMAND Short-run technology that permits the printing of the quantities needed at the time they are needed.

PUBLICATION DATE The official date when a book is published and therefore is for sale.

Examination copies may be distributed before this date.

PUBNET An electronic ordering system developed by the Higher Education Division of the ASSOCIATION OF AMERICAN PUBLISHERS.

ROYALTIES A set percentage of net sales paid to authors. Sometimes royalties are established on a sliding scale ("jump royalties") that increases with sales.

RUNNING HEAD The title of the book, part, or chapter across the top of each page. When placed at the bottom, they are called running feet.

SERIF or SANS SERIF TYPEFACE The presence or absence in a typeface of a short decorative line. *Compare* Century Schoolbook *and* Helvetica.

SEWN, or SMYTHE-SEWN, BINDING A binding in which SIGNATURES are stitched together.

SHEETS Paper, cut into squares or rectangles.

SIGNATURE A set of pages—usually 32, but sometimes 16 or 8—printed at the same time, then folded for binding.

SPECIFICATIONS The physical characteristics of a product—for a book, includes the trim size, number of pages, number of colors, binding, etc.

SUPPLEMENTS Independent materials used in addition to the core educational product in a course, such as a reader. *Compare* ANCILLARIES.

TRIM SIZE The physical dimensions of a book.

INDEX